How Long, O Lord?

How Long, O Lord?

Preaching Scripture in a Wounded World

G. C. SMITH

RESOURCE *Publications* • Eugene, Oregon

HOW LONG, O LORD?
Preaching Scripture in a Wounded World

Resource Publications
An Imprint of Wipf and Stock Publishers
199 W. 8th Ave., Suite 3
Eugene, OR 97401

www.wipfandstock.com

PAPERBACK ISBN: 979-8-3852-8257-9
HARDCOVER ISBN: 979-8-3852-8258-6
EBOOK ISBN: 979-8-3852-8259-3

VERSION NUMBER 04/22/26

Unless otherwise indicated, all reflections, interpretations, and theological conclusions are those of the author.

This book is intended for educational and pastoral use. It is not a substitute for professional mental health care. Readers experiencing acute distress are encouraged to seek appropriate professional support.

"How long, O Lord? Will you forget me forever?"

—Psalm 13:1

Contents

Preface

This book grew out of a simple pastoral question that surfaces again and again in ministry:

How do we preach faithfully when the world no longer seems to make moral sense?

Pastors regularly sit with people who carry deep wounds. They have experienced suffering, injustice, betrayal, or loss that appears to contradict what they believe about God and the way the world is supposed to work. In those moments the question is not merely emotional. It is moral. People feel that something in the moral structure of their world has broken.

In recent years this experience has come to be described as moral injury. Although the term is modern, the experience is not. The Bible repeatedly gives voice to individuals and communities who confront moments when the moral order of the world appears to collapse. Job's suffering, the cries of lament in the Psalms, the devastation of exile, and the cry of Jesus from the cross all testify that Scripture does not avoid these moments. It preserves them.

This book is written for preaching pastors who want to engage these texts more honestly and preach them more faithfully.

Each chapter focuses on a biblical passage that confronts the breaking of the moral world. The chapters follow a consistent pattern: we begin by considering how the passage is often preached, then ask a diagnostic question—Where does the moral world appear to break in this text? From there we explore what becomes visible when the passage is read through the lens of moral injury. Each chapter concludes with a sermon demonstrating how this insight can shape preaching.

The goal is not simply to offer new interpretations of familiar passages. The goal is to help pastors rediscover something that Scripture already contains: a profound honesty about suffering, injustice, and the apparent collapse of the moral world—and the good news that God meets humanity even there.

If this book helps pastors preach with greater honesty, deeper compassion, and renewed confidence in the gospel, it will have served its purpose.

Introduction

Preaching When the World No Longer Makes Sense

THE MORAL WOUNDS PEOPLE BRING INTO CHURCH

Every pastor eventually hears the same kind of question.

Sometimes it is asked directly. A person may sit across from you in the quiet of your office and say, "Pastor, I don't understand how this could happen." At other times the question emerges more indirectly through grief, frustration, or confusion—a hospital room conversation, a phone call after midnight, or a quiet moment in the hallway after worship.

The question rarely sounds philosophical. It is not framed as a theological debate or an intellectual puzzle. Instead it rises from lived experience.

Why did this happen?
Where was God?
How can the world work like this?

Behind questions like these lies something deeper than curiosity. Often what people are expressing is the painful realization that the world no longer seems to operate according to the moral expectations they once trusted.

A child dies unexpectedly. A faithful marriage collapses. A person who devoted their life to serving others becomes gravely ill. A trusted leader betrays those who depended on them. A community experiences violence that leaves everyone asking how such cruelty could exist.

Moments like these wound the human spirit in a particular way. They do not merely cause sorrow or fear. They disrupt the moral framework through which people understand reality. Something about the way the world is supposed to work appears to have broken.

In recent years scholars and psychologists have begun to use a term for this experience: moral injury.

The phrase originally emerged in discussions about soldiers returning from war. Many veterans were not only struggling with trauma but with the realization that they had witnessed or participated in events that violated their deepest moral convictions. What haunted them was not merely danger or loss but the sense that the moral structure of their world had fractured.

Although the language is relatively new, the experience is not limited to soldiers or extreme situations. Moral injury can arise whenever people encounter events that violate the moral expectations they once trusted.

For some, the wound emerges from personal tragedy. A person who believed that faithfulness would lead to blessing suddenly confronts devastating loss. For others, the injury arises from witnessing injustice in the world around them. Someone who believes goodness matters sees cruelty rewarded and corruption flourish.

In both cases the result can be the same: the unsettling sense that the moral order of the world no longer makes sense.

Pastors encounter these experiences constantly.

People rarely use the phrase moral injury when they describe their pain. Instead they speak in simpler language:

"I thought God would protect us."
"I tried to do the right thing."
"I prayed and nothing changed."

"I don't understand why this happened."

These statements reveal the deeper struggle beneath the grief. People are not only mourning what they have lost. They are struggling to understand how the world can function in ways that appear to contradict everything they believed about God, justice, and the meaning of faith.

And yet many churches struggle to speak about these experiences honestly.

Congregations gather each week with people carrying moral wounds, but sermons often assume a world that still feels morally coherent. We speak about faith, obedience, and hope as though the structure of the world remains intact.

For those whose lives feel fractured, this disconnect can be painful.

The Bible promises that God is just. It proclaims that righteousness matters. It insists that God is faithful to the covenant. But when life seems to contradict those convictions, people long for language that allows them to speak honestly about what they are experiencing.

They want to know whether Scripture has room for their questions.
They want to know whether faith allows them to voice their confusion.
They want to know whether the church can acknowledge that sometimes the world simply does not make sense.

Surprisingly, the Bible answers these questions with a resounding yes.

Scripture is filled with voices that speak from precisely these moments of moral rupture. The Bible preserves prayers that protest injustice, stories that wrestle with undeserved suffering, and poems that cry out in confusion when God seems absent.

Faith in the Bible never requires pretending that the world always behaves as it should.

Instead Scripture preserves the voices of people who brought their deepest questions before God.

When pastors recognize this dimension of the biblical story, they discover something important: the moral wounds people carry into church are not foreign to Scripture.

They are already there.

The challenge is learning how to preach these texts in ways that allow their honesty to be heard.

But before exploring how such preaching works, we must first consider an important question. If Scripture speaks so honestly about suffering and injustice, why do so many sermons move quickly past those themes?

The answer reveals something important about the way many of us have learned to read and preach the Bible.

WHY MANY SERMONS MISS THE REALITY PEOPLE LIVE IN

Most pastors enter ministry because they love Scripture and care deeply about the people entrusted to them. They want their preaching to bring hope, clarity, and spiritual nourishment. Week after week they labor over the biblical text, searching for ways to communicate its truth in ways that strengthen faith.

Yet despite these sincere intentions, many sermons quietly miss the emotional and moral world people are actually living in.

This rarely happens because pastors are unaware of suffering. In fact, pastors often witness more human pain than almost anyone else in the congregation. They sit with families in hospital rooms, counsel couples whose marriages are collapsing, and walk with people through grief, betrayal, addiction, and loss.

The difficulty usually lies elsewhere.

It often emerges from the habits of interpretation pastors have been taught. In many churches preaching follows a familiar pattern: the preacher studies a passage, identifies its central message, explains its theological meaning, and applies that meaning to everyday life.

This method has real strengths. Congregations benefit from sermons that are clear, organized, and grounded in the biblical text. People need guidance about how faith shapes their decisions and relationships.

But there is also a subtle danger hidden within this pattern.

When sermons move too quickly toward explanation and application, they can bypass the very tension the biblical text is trying to expose.

Many passages of Scripture do not resolve questions immediately. Instead they invite readers into moments of confusion, protest, grief, or moral disorientation. These texts preserve the voices of people struggling to understand how their faith fits within a world that appears to contradict their deepest convictions.

Yet sermons often smooth out these tensions.

A psalm of lament becomes a lesson about trusting God during difficult times. The story of Job becomes encouragement to remain patient in suffering. The crucifixion becomes primarily a theological explanation of salvation rather than a moment when the moral order of the world appears to collapse.

These interpretations are not necessarily wrong.

They simply move too quickly.

They arrive at resolution before acknowledging the depth of the crisis the biblical text is describing.

As a result, sermons sometimes speak a different language than the lives people are actually living.

Someone who has endured devastating loss may come to church hoping to hear something that speaks honestly to the confusion they feel. Instead they hear reassurance that God has a plan and that everything will ultimately work together for good.

While such statements may contain truth, they can feel strangely disconnected from the experience of someone whose world has been shattered.

Learning to preach Scripture faithfully therefore requires patience. It requires allowing the tension within the text to remain visible long enough for people to recognize their own experience within it.

When pastors learn to do this, something remarkable happens.

The Bible begins to sound more like the world people are actually living in.

THE BIBLE'S HONEST LANGUAGE OF MORAL COLLAPSE

One of the most surprising discoveries pastors make when they begin reading Scripture through the lens of moral injury is how frequently the Bible speaks about moments when the moral order of the world appears to collapse.

Many Christians associate the Bible primarily with faith, obedience, redemption, and hope. These themes are certainly present and central to the biblical story. Yet alongside them runs another powerful current: the language of protest, lament, confusion, and moral disorientation.

Scripture repeatedly preserves the voices of people struggling to understand how the world can function in ways that seem to contradict everything they believe about God.

These voices appear throughout the biblical narrative.

In the Psalms, worshipers cry out:

"How long, O Lord?"
"Why do the wicked prosper?"
"My God, my God, why have you forsaken me?"

These prayers arise from the experience of moral rupture. The worshiper believes God is just and faithful, yet the world appears to contradict those convictions.

The psalmist does not hide this tension. The tension becomes the prayer itself.

The book of Job explores this crisis with extraordinary intensity. Job begins the story as a man who embodies everything Israel's moral tradition associates with blessing. Yet his world suddenly collapses. His children die, his wealth disappears, and his health deteriorates.

Job's friends insist that suffering must be the result of wrongdoing. But Job refuses their explanation. He insists that the moral logic they defend no longer explains his experience.

The narrative allows his protest to unfold across dozens of chapters, inviting readers to feel the weight of his confusion.

The prophets express similar tensions. Jeremiah cries out, "Why does the way of the wicked prosper?" (Jer 12:1). He witnesses corruption and injustice in the society he is called to confront and brings that confusion directly to God.

The poetry of Lamentations gives voice to a community whose world has collapsed after Jerusalem's destruction. The temple is gone, the monarchy has fallen, and the people wander in exile.

Even the New Testament continues this pattern.

The Gospels portray Jesus encountering people whose lives have been broken by suffering, injustice, and exclusion. His ministry confronts the brokenness of the present world.

Yet the experience of moral collapse reaches its most dramatic moment at the cross.

From the perspective of Jesus' followers, the crucifixion represents the complete failure of their expectations. The one they believed to be the Messiah is rejected and executed.

At the center of the scene stands Jesus crying out the first words of Psalm 22:

"My God, my God, why have you forsaken me?"

The resurrection does not erase the cross. Instead it transforms its meaning.

The Bible therefore contains a remarkable honesty about the experience of faith. It acknowledges that believers often encounter moments when the moral order of the world appears to break.

Rather than hiding those moments, Scripture preserves them.

HOW MORAL INJURY CHANGES THE WAY WE READ SCRIPTURE

Recognizing this pattern changes the way the Bible is read.

Stories that once seemed isolated begin to appear connected. Laments that once felt uncomfortable begin to sound like the natural language of faith in a broken world.

Reading Scripture through the lens of moral injury asks a simple question:

Where does the moral world appear to break in this passage?

This question highlights tensions already present in the text but often minimized in preaching.

The story of Job becomes a crisis of moral understanding rather than simply a lesson about perseverance. The lament psalms become moral protest. The ministry of Jesus becomes a confrontation with the broken moral structure of the world.

The cross becomes the ultimate moment of moral collapse.

Yet the resurrection reveals that God has entered that collapse and begun restoring the world.

Recognizing this pattern allows pastors to read Scripture with fresh clarity.

Again and again the biblical story follows a similar movement:

Covenant expectation.
Moral rupture.
Lament and protest.
Divine restoration.

Understanding this pattern transforms preaching.

Hope then emerges not by ignoring suffering but by discovering that God meets humanity in the very places where the moral order appears to collapse.

THE CENTRAL CLAIM OF THIS BOOK

At the heart of this book is a simple conviction:

Many biblical passages pastors preach every week are best understood as responses to moments when the moral order of the world appears to collapse.

When these passages are read through the lens of moral injury, their meaning becomes clearer and their relevance to modern congregations becomes unmistakable.

The Bible repeatedly confronts moments when believers discover that the world does not behave the way they expected.

The righteous suffer.
The wicked prosper.
God appears silent.
Promises seem delayed.

When these moments occur, the people of God must decide how to interpret their experience.

The biblical writers place this struggle at the center of the story.

The crucifixion represents the ultimate moral rupture.

Yet the resurrection reveals that God has entered the place where the world seemed most broken.

This book explores how recognizing that pattern changes the way Scripture is read and preached.

Each chapter focuses on a biblical passage, beginning with a pastoral scenario, examining the common interpretation, asking where the moral world breaks, and demonstrating how that discovery reshapes the sermon.

The goal is deeply practical.

Pastors who read Scripture through the lens of moral injury often discover that their sermons become more honest, more compassionate, and more connected to the experiences people carry into church each week.

Instead of avoiding the hardest questions, preaching can bring them into conversation with the biblical story.

Instead of pretending that the world always makes sense, sermons can acknowledge the moments when it does not.

And instead of offering hope that bypasses suffering, the gospel can be proclaimed as the good news that God meets humanity precisely where the moral world appears to break.

In a world where many people feel that the moral structure of life has fractured, that kind of preaching is not merely helpful.

It is necessary.

Recognizing the language of moral rupture in Scripture is therefore only the first step. Pastors must also learn how to identify when that dynamic is present in a biblical passage. Not every text contains lament or protest, and the tension is sometimes subtle.

If the moral injury lens is to become a practical tool for preaching rather than simply an interesting idea, preachers need a way to recognize these moments in the text.

The following section offers a simple diagnostic guide that helps pastors do exactly that.

A Diagnostic Tool for Preachers

How to Recognize Moral Injury in Scripture

One of the most practical questions pastors ask when they encounter a new interpretive lens is simple: How do I actually use this when preparing a sermon?

The language of moral injury can sound compelling in theory. It resonates with the experiences people carry into church, and it appears repeatedly in Scripture. But when a pastor sits down with a biblical text on Monday morning, the task is concrete. The preacher must determine what the passage is saying and how it should be proclaimed.

This book proposes that many passages become clearer when we ask a series of diagnostic questions that help us recognize moments of moral rupture within the text. These questions are not complicated. They do not require advanced technical tools or specialized academic training. Instead, they simply guide our attention toward features of Scripture that are often present but easily overlooked.

The five questions below can help pastors discern when a passage is engaging the kind of moral collapse that produces moral injury.

DOES THE TEXT ASSUME THE WORLD SHOULD MAKE MORAL SENSE?

The first step in recognizing moral injury in Scripture is identifying whether the text assumes that the world should operate according to a moral order.

The Bible consistently presents reality as morally structured. From the earliest chapters of Genesis through the teachings of Jesus, the story assumes that the world is not random or indifferent. Instead, it is created and sustained by a God whose character is just, faithful, and good.

Because of this conviction, biblical writers often assume that moral behavior and moral outcomes should correspond.

Faithfulness should lead to blessing.
Justice should prevail over injustice.
The righteous should ultimately flourish.

These assumptions appear clearly in passages such as Deuteronomy 30, where obedience to God is associated with life and prosperity, while disobedience leads to hardship. Similar expectations appear throughout the wisdom literature, particularly in the book of Proverbs, which repeatedly affirms that righteousness leads to life while wickedness leads to ruin.

When a biblical text begins from these kinds of assumptions, it establishes the moral framework within which moral injury can occur.

If the world is expected to make moral sense, then events that contradict that expectation will feel profoundly disruptive.

Pastors who recognize this framework begin to see that many biblical passages are built upon a moral vision of reality. The writers assume that the world should reflect the justice and faithfulness of God.

This expectation forms the backdrop for the tensions that follow.

DOES THE PASSAGE DESCRIBE THE COLLAPSE OF MORAL ORDER?

The second diagnostic question moves directly to the heart of moral injury:

Does the passage describe a moment when the moral order of the world appears to break?

These moments occur when events contradict the expectations established by the covenantal worldview. The righteous suffer while the wicked prosper. Justice fails. Innocent people are harmed while corrupt individuals flourish.

The Bible contains many such moments.

Job loses everything despite living a life of integrity. The psalmists repeatedly ask why the wicked seem to prosper while the faithful struggle. The destruction of Jerusalem in 586 BCE shatters the institutions through which Israel understood God's presence.

The crucifixion of Jesus represents perhaps the most dramatic example. The one proclaimed as the Messiah is rejected, condemned, and executed while those responsible for his death appear to triumph.

Each of these moments represents a breakdown of the moral expectations that shaped the community's understanding of reality.

Recognizing this collapse is crucial for interpretation.

If pastors overlook the moral rupture within a passage, they may misidentify the central tension of the text. The passage may appear to be offering a simple lesson about patience, perseverance, or obedience. But once the collapse of moral order is recognized, the deeper question becomes visible.

How can faith survive when the world no longer behaves as it should?

DOES THE TEXT GIVE VOICE TO PROTEST OR LAMENT?

When moral expectations collapse, the natural human response is often protest.

The Bible preserves this response with remarkable honesty. Rather than suppressing it, Scripture repeatedly allows believers to bring their confusion, anger, and grief before God.

This is especially visible in the lament psalms.

Psalm 13 opens with the cry, "How long, O Lord? Will you forget me forever?" Psalm 22 begins with the haunting question, "My God, my God, why have you forsaken me?" These prayers do not disguise the emotional intensity of the speaker's experience. They confront God directly with the apparent failure of justice.

The same pattern appears in the book of Job, where Job refuses to accept the explanations offered by his friends and demands that God respond to his questions.

Prophetic literature also contains moments of protest. Jeremiah questions why the wicked prosper. Habakkuk cries out in confusion as he witnesses violence and injustice.

These texts reveal something profound about biblical faith: protest is not the opposite of belief.

In many cases, protest arises precisely because the speaker takes God's promises seriously. If God has committed to justice, then injustice demands an explanation.

Pastors who learn to recognize the language of protest and lament begin to see that these voices form a central part of the biblical tradition. They represent the emotional and spiritual response of believers who encounter moral rupture.

Ignoring these voices can unintentionally silence one of the most honest dimensions of Scripture.

DOES THE PASSAGE RESIST EASY EXPLANATIONS?

Another important signal of moral injury within a biblical text is the presence of unresolved tension.

Many passages resist attempts to provide simple explanations for suffering or injustice. Instead, they invite readers to remain within the tension created by the collapse of moral expectations.

The book of Job offers a clear example. Job's friends insist that suffering must result from sin. Their arguments follow a familiar theological pattern: if the world is morally ordered, then wrongdoing must explain suffering.

Yet the narrative itself undermines their reasoning. The reader knows from the beginning that Job's suffering is not a punishment for wrongdoing. The traditional explanation fails.

Even when God eventually speaks from the whirlwind, the divine response does not provide the kind of tidy explanation the reader might expect. Instead, God points to the vast complexity of creation.

The book concludes without resolving every question raised by Job's suffering.

This resistance to easy answers appears in other parts of Scripture as well. The lament psalms often end with hope, but they rarely explain why the suffering occurred. The prophets interpret historical catastrophe as judgment, yet they also express profound grief and confusion.

These unresolved tensions remind us that the Bible does not always attempt to explain suffering fully.

Instead, it allows the questions to remain visible.

For preachers, this recognition can be liberating. It means sermons do not need to eliminate every tension within a passage. Sometimes faithful preaching involves acknowledging the mystery rather than resolving it.

DOES THE TEXT REVEAL GOD PRESENT WITHIN THE RUPTURE?

The final diagnostic question brings us to the heart of the gospel:

Where is God in the midst of the moral rupture?

The Bible rarely denies the reality of suffering or injustice. Instead, it repeatedly reveals that God meets people within those moments of collapse.

In the lament psalms, the very act of prayer assumes that God is still listening. In Job, God eventually responds to Job's protest. In the prophetic writings, promises of restoration emerge even in the midst of exile.

The ultimate expression of this pattern appears in the story of Jesus.

The cross represents the deepest moral rupture in the biblical narrative. The innocent one is condemned. The Messiah is rejected. The world appears to have chosen violence over truth.

Yet Christians confess that God was present precisely in that moment.

The resurrection does not erase the rupture of the cross. Instead, it reveals that God has entered into the brokenness of the world in order to redeem it.

Recognizing this pattern transforms the way pastors preach difficult passages.

The sermon does not need to deny the collapse of moral order. Instead, it can acknowledge the rupture honestly while proclaiming the presence of God within it.

This is the distinctive hope of the Christian gospel.

God does not remain distant from the moral wounds of the world.

God enters them.

These five questions provide a simple diagnostic tool for pastors preparing sermons.

They help identify when a passage is engaging the experience of moral rupture and guide the preacher toward the deeper tensions present within the text.

As we move into the chapters that follow, these questions will serve as our interpretive compass. Each passage we examine will reveal how the moral injury lens can illuminate familiar texts in ways that speak powerfully to the world people inhabit today.

And in each case, the goal remains the same: to preach Scripture in a way that acknowledges the moral wounds people carry while proclaiming the hope that God meets us precisely there.

PART I

WHEN THE MORAL WORLD BEGINS TO BREAK

Chapter 1

Covenant Expectations and the Moral Order

Scripture: Deuteronomy 30

OPENING PASTORAL SCENARIO

Every pastor eventually encounters a moment when the usual answers no longer seem sufficient.

Sometimes it happens in a hospital room where a family waits quietly for news they never expected to hear. Sometimes it comes after a funeral, when grief begins to give way to deeper questions. Sometimes it emerges during a pastoral conversation when someone finally voices the confusion they have carried for weeks.

The question often sounds simple.

"Why did this happen?"

Yet beneath that question lies something deeper than a request for explanation. The person asking is not only trying to understand a painful event. They are struggling to understand how the world itself is supposed to work.

A faithful church member loses a spouse after years of prayer. A devoted parent watches a child drift away from the values they worked so hard to teach. A family that has served their community with generosity suddenly faces a tragedy that feels profoundly unfair.

In moments like these people are not simply grieving a loss. They are wrestling with the unsettling possibility that the world may not function according to the moral order they trusted.

Today this experience is often described as moral injury.

The phrase first appeared in conversations with soldiers who had witnessed events that shattered their deepest moral assumptions. The wound they carried was not only emotional or psychological but spiritual. Something about their experience violated the framework through which they had previously understood right and wrong.

Over time it became clear that moral injury is not limited to the battlefield. It can arise whenever events contradict the moral vision people trust.

Betrayal can produce moral injury.
Profound injustice can produce moral injury.
A tragedy that appears undeserved can produce moral injury.

In each case the deepest wound is not simply suffering but the collapse of moral meaning. The assumptions that once made life feel coherent and trustworthy no longer seem reliable.

Pastors encounter this struggle frequently, even if it is not always named.

Members of a congregation rarely use the phrase moral injury, but they often describe the experience clearly. They say things like:

"I thought if I tried to live faithfully things would turn out differently."

"I don't understand why God would allow this."

"This just doesn't seem right."

Behind these statements lies a powerful conviction: the world should make moral sense.

People believe goodness should matter. Faithfulness should matter. Justice should matter. If someone sincerely tries to live well and honor God, life should reflect those commitments.

When events appear to contradict that expectation, the confusion reaches deeper than ordinary grief.

Pastors feel this tension as well. When someone asks why tragedy has entered their life, we feel the weight of the question. We want to comfort them. We want to reassure them that God remains faithful even in suffering.

Often we respond by offering explanations.

We may say suffering builds character.
We may say God has a hidden purpose.
We may say everything happens for a reason.

While these responses may contain elements of truth, they sometimes fail to address the deeper question being asked. The person sitting before us is not simply asking why suffering exists. They are asking how suffering fits within a world governed by a just and faithful God.

This helps clarify why sermons sometimes fail to connect with lived experience in the congregation. Preaching can quietly assume that life already makes sense. The message encourages people to trust God and live faithfully, yet it may not address the deeper tension many listeners carry.

People in the pews are not always looking for encouragement alone. Often they are trying to reconcile their faith with experiences that feel morally confusing. They believe in God's goodness but struggle to understand how that goodness relates to what they have endured.

It is precisely here that passages like Deuteronomy 30 become important.

Before Scripture wrestles openly with suffering, injustice, and confusion, it first describes the moral vision through which life was meant to unfold.

Deuteronomy 30 presents that vision clearly. The covenant describes a world in which faithfulness leads toward life and where human choices matter because they unfold within the moral order established by God.

Understanding this vision is essential, because the rest of Scripture will repeatedly return to moments when that moral order appears to fracture.

Before Scripture wrestles openly with suffering, injustice, and confusion, it first describes the moral vision through which life was meant to unfold.

Deuteronomy 30 presents a world where faithfulness leads to life, where obedience produces blessing, and where the order of reality reflects the character of God himself.

Understanding that vision is the first step toward understanding the deeper tensions that unfold throughout the rest of Scripture.

THE PASSAGE AS WE USUALLY PREACH IT

Deuteronomy 30 has long served as a powerful passage for preaching about obedience and decision.

Near the end of his life, Moses gathers the people of Israel and summarizes the covenant that has defined their relationship with God. After recounting God's faithfulness and reminding the people of the commands given at Sinai, he presents a dramatic contrast:

"I have set before you life and death, blessing and curse. Therefore choose life" (verse 19).

Many sermons on this passage emphasize the responsibility of the people to choose obedience. God has revealed the path of life, and the community must decide whether they will walk in it.

Within this framework, Deuteronomy 30 becomes a call to commitment. The preacher invites listeners to renew their dedication to God, reminding them that the choices they make shape the direction of their lives.

This approach resonates naturally with the way most people already think about the world. We instinctively believe that good decisions lead to good outcomes. Integrity should lead toward stability. Faithfulness should lead toward blessing.

In this sense sermons based on Deuteronomy 30 reinforce a moral expectation that already exists in the human heart.

Life should make sense.

If someone lives faithfully, honors God, and treats others justly, their life should reflect those commitments. Reality should reward righteousness and expose wrongdoing.

This expectation runs deep within human experience. Parents teach it to their children. Teachers reinforce it in classrooms. Communities depend on it to maintain trust and cooperation.

Scripture itself often affirms this vision. Throughout the Old Testament, covenant language connects obedience with blessing and disobedience with destruction. Faithfulness leads toward life, while rebellion leads toward loss.

Deuteronomy 30 expresses this covenant logic clearly. The people are invited to choose life by loving God, walking in his ways, and keeping his commandments. If they do, the community will flourish in the land God has given them.

In sermons this message often becomes an invitation to spiritual renewal. The preacher encourages listeners to recommit themselves to God, to choose the path of obedience, and to trust that such faithfulness leads toward life.

There is genuine wisdom in this approach. Scripture consistently affirms that faithfulness matters. Choices matter. The direction of a life carries consequences.

Yet once this expectation is established, a difficult question begins to surface.

What happens when reality does not follow this pattern?

Many people listening to sermons already know that life does not always unfold in the way these expectations suggest. They have watched faithful Christians endure devastating illness. They have seen generous people betrayed. They have witnessed tragedies that seem morally inexplicable.

When these experiences collide with sermons that strongly emphasize the connection between obedience and blessing, listeners may feel a troubling tension.

If faithfulness leads to life, why does my life feel so broken?

If obedience brings blessing, why has my family suffered so deeply?

Without intending to, sermons can intensify the confusion people already carry. The preacher affirms the moral vision of the covenant, but the listener may quietly wonder why their own experience seems to contradict it.

This tension is not new. In fact, it lies near the center of the biblical story itself.

Many of Scripture's most powerful passages arise from the struggle to understand why life sometimes contradicts the moral vision established by the covenant.

The psalmists cry out when injustice flourishes.
The prophets lament corruption that overwhelms the land.
The wisdom writers wrestle with the suffering of the righteous.

These texts reveal that the tension between moral expectation and lived experience is not a minor theme in the Bible. It is one of the central struggles of faith.

The covenant vision described in passages like Deuteronomy 30 presents a world that reflects the justice of God and affirms that human choices matter.

But once that vision shapes the imagination of the people, experiences of injustice or undeserved suffering become deeply unsettling.

When reality seems to contradict the justice God promises, believers are forced to ask difficult questions about how the world truly works.

These questions do not arise from unbelief. They arise from faith.

People ask them precisely because they believe the world should reflect the character of God.

Scripture does not silence these questions. Instead, it preserves them. The Bible allows the voices of those who struggle with moral confusion to speak honestly before God.

Recognizing this tension prepares us to ask a crucial interpretive question as we read the text:

Where does the moral world appear to break?

That question will guide the next stage of our reading.

THE MORAL INJURY QUESTION

This leads to an important interpretive question for preachers:

Where does the moral world appear to break?

When we read Scripture carefully, we discover that many biblical passages emerge from moments when the moral coherence of life appears to fracture. Events occur that seem incompatible with the character of God and the expectations created by faith.

The covenant language of Deuteronomy 30 presents a morally coherent vision of reality. Blessing follows faithfulness, while disobedience leads toward destruction. The world is portrayed as a place where moral choices matter and where their consequences unfold within the order established by God.

Yet once that vision shapes the imagination of the people, experiences that contradict it become deeply unsettling.

What happens when the righteous suffer?

What happens when injustice flourishes without consequence?

What happens when tragedy strikes those who have tried to live faithfully?

These moments represent more than ordinary suffering. They reveal an experience of moral rupture.

When believers encounter events that contradict their deepest expectations about how the world should work, confusion reaches into the heart of faith itself. The problem is not simply that life is painful. The problem is that life suddenly seems morally disordered.

This experience is often described as moral injury.

Moral injury occurs when events violate the moral framework through which a person understands reality. The wound is not only emotional pain but the collapse of meaning itself. What once seemed morally stable suddenly feels uncertain.

In many ways the covenant vision of Deuteronomy prepares the ground for this experience. By declaring that life flows from faithfulness and destruction from disobedience, it establishes powerful expectations about how the world should behave.

When life appears to contradict those expectations, believers struggle to reconcile their experience with the vision of reality they trust.

This struggle appears repeatedly throughout Scripture.

The psalmists cry out when injustice seems to go unanswered. They describe situations in which the wicked prosper while the faithful suffer.

The prophets confront societies in which violence, corruption, and oppression dominate public life. Their protests arise from the conviction that such conditions contradict the justice of God.

The wisdom literature explores the tension even more deeply. The book of Job presents a righteous man whose life collapses without any clear moral explanation. Job's suffering cannot easily be reconciled with the moral logic many assume governs the world.

What is striking about these texts is their honesty.

Rather than suppressing moral confusion, Scripture preserves it. The Bible does not pretend that faith eliminates the experience of contradiction. Instead, it allows the voices of those who struggle to remain visible within the story of God's people.

This honesty distinguishes the biblical tradition.

Many religious systems attempt to maintain harmony by minimizing doubt or discouraging difficult questions. Scripture often moves in the opposite direction. It gives language to protest, lament, and confusion.

Believers cry out to God when life no longer makes sense.

These cries are not expressions of unbelief. They arise precisely because the faithful believe the world should reflect the justice of God.

When reality appears to violate that expectation, believers bring their confusion directly into conversation with God.

Recognizing this pattern helps us see why the question of moral rupture is so important when interpreting Scripture.

Many biblical passages are not simply teaching abstract theological ideas. They arise from moments when believers struggle to understand how God's justice relates to the realities they are experiencing.

When we read the text with this awareness, new dimensions begin to appear.

We begin to notice where the covenant's moral vision collides with lived experience. We hear the voices of people trying to interpret their suffering within the framework of faith.

Scripture refuses to ignore these tensions.

Instead of offering quick explanations, the biblical tradition often lingers within the confusion. The struggle itself becomes part of the ongoing conversation between God and the community.

For preachers, recognizing this dynamic is crucial.

If we assume that Scripture always presents a simple and stable moral world, we may overlook the deeper struggles many passages address. We may preach texts as though they offer straightforward answers when they are actually wrestling with difficult questions.

But when we ask where the moral world appears to break, we begin to read the Bible more attentively.

We notice the moments when faith confronts suffering, injustice, and confusion. We hear the voices of those who bring their wounded expectations before God.

And in doing so we discover that the Bible speaks with remarkable honesty about the tensions believers continue to experience today.

WHAT THE MORAL INJURY LENS REVEALS

When we read Deuteronomy 30 through the lens of moral injury, something important becomes visible.

The covenant does more than give commands. It reveals the kind of world God intends.

Moses' words to Israel describe a moral universe in which life unfolds within a coherent relationship between faithfulness and flourishing. The covenant invites the people to walk in God's ways and assures them that such faithfulness leads toward life.

"I have set before you life and death, blessing and curse. Therefore choose life."

This declaration expresses more than moral instruction. It reflects a vision of reality itself. The world God creates is not morally chaotic but ordered in a way that reflects the character of its Creator.

In this vision goodness matters. Justice matters. Faithfulness matters. Human choices are not arbitrary acts but participate in the moral order established by God.

The covenant therefore portrays a world where life and blessing are connected to the character of God and the practices of his people. Obedience leads toward life because it aligns human life with the purposes of God.

Yet once believers embrace this vision, they inevitably encounter moments when reality appears to contradict it.

People expect justice to prevail, yet they witness corruption and exploitation.

They expect righteousness to bring stability, yet they see faithful people endure profound suffering.

They expect goodness to be rewarded, yet they encounter situations where evil appears to prosper.

When such contradictions appear, the tension becomes deeply unsettling.

Something about the world feels wrong.

This reaction is not merely emotional. It reflects a moral intuition shaped by the covenant itself. Believers sense that reality is not functioning in the way God intended.

Seen from this perspective, the experience of moral injury becomes easier to understand.

The covenant teaches that the world possesses a moral order grounded in the character of God. When events appear to violate that order, believers experience a rupture in their understanding of reality.

They are not only grieving or confused. They are struggling to interpret how the world can reflect God's justice while containing experiences that seem profoundly unjust.

This insight helps explain why Scripture contains so many voices of lament and protest.

The psalmists cry out when injustice goes unanswered.

The prophets protest societies that abandon justice and compassion.

The wisdom writers wrestle with the mystery of suffering.

Rather than ignoring the tension between moral expectation and lived experience, Scripture preserves the voices of those who struggle with it.

The Bible allows believers to speak honestly about moments when life no longer seems to make sense.

This honesty is one of the most distinctive features of the biblical witness.

Believers cry out to God when they encounter injustice.

They question the meaning of suffering.
They lament the apparent absence of divine intervention.

Yet these cries are not expressions of faithlessness.

They arise from the conviction that the world should reflect the justice and goodness of God.

Lament grows out of covenant faith.

People protest because they believe God is just. They lament because they believe the world should reflect that justice.

When events contradict that expectation, the faithful do not abandon their belief. Instead, they bring their confusion into conversation with God.

This dynamic reveals something profound about the nature of biblical faith.

Faith does not require the denial of moral confusion. Instead, it creates a relationship in which believers can confront that confusion honestly.

The covenant invites the people to walk with God, and that relationship includes moments of tension and struggle.

Believers continue to trust God even when they cannot fully understand how the events of their lives fit within the moral vision they believe in.

HOW THIS CHANGES THE SERMON

Recognizing the tension between covenant expectation and lived experience changes the way a passage like Deuteronomy 30 can be preached.

Traditionally sermons on this text emphasize the call to obedience. The preacher highlights the responsibility of God's people to choose life by loving the Lord, walking in his ways, and keeping his commandments.

The passage becomes an invitation to renewal.

There is much to affirm in this approach. Scripture consistently teaches that faithfulness matters. Our choices matter. The direction of our lives is not morally neutral.

Yet when this message is presented without acknowledging the deeper tensions of human experience, it can leave some listeners feeling unseen.

Many people sitting in church have already tried to live faithfully. They have prayed, served, and sought to honor God with their lives. Yet their experiences may not reflect the pattern of blessing they expected.

They have encountered illness that prayer did not prevent.

They have endured losses that seem deeply unfair.

They have watched injustice unfold in ways that defy explanation.

When sermons confidently emphasize the connection between obedience and blessing without acknowledging these realities, listeners may begin to feel isolated in their struggle.

Some may quietly wonder whether something is wrong with their faith. Others may assume their suffering reflects hidden failure.

The moral injury lens invites the preacher to approach this passage differently.

Instead of presenting the covenant as a formula for success, the sermon can recognize that Deuteronomy 30 describes the world God intends. It offers a vision of life in which faithfulness leads toward flourishing and where reality reflects the character of God.

This vision is not naïve. It reflects the biblical conviction that creation is ordered toward justice and life.

At the same time the preacher can acknowledge that human experience does not always appear to follow this pattern.

Scripture itself bears witness to that tension.

The psalmists cry out when injustice flourishes.

The prophets protest corruption and oppression.

The wisdom writers wrestle with the suffering of the righteous.

These voices show that God's people have long struggled to reconcile faith in a just God with the painful realities of the world.

Recognizing this tension does not weaken the message of Deuteronomy 30. It deepens it.

The covenant does not promise that life will always unfold according to simple formulas. Instead, it reveals the moral vision of the world God created and the life God invites his people to embrace.

Choosing life means aligning oneself with the purposes of God even when the path forward is not fully clear.

This perspective allows the sermon to speak honestly about the experiences people bring into church each week.

Listeners do not need to pretend that life always makes sense. They do not need to hide their questions or suppress their confusion.

The biblical tradition itself gives voice to those struggles.

When the preacher acknowledges this truth, the message of Deuteronomy 30 becomes more than a call to moral decision.

It becomes an invitation to trust the goodness of God even when the world feels uncertain.

Choosing life does not mean pretending that suffering is easy to explain. It means trusting that the God who created the world for life and blessing remains faithful even when the path of faith is difficult to understand.

This kind of preaching creates space for honesty within the congregation.

People who carry questions about suffering and injustice no longer feel as though their struggles disqualify them from faith. Instead they recognize that their questions place them within the long story of believers who have wrestled with the same tensions.

Faith becomes not the denial of confusion but the decision to remain in relationship with God in the midst of it.

When Deuteronomy 30 is preached in this way, the passage speaks directly to the moral struggles many people experience today.

It reminds the congregation that the world God intends is shaped by life, justice, and blessing.

It acknowledges that the present world often falls short of that vision.

And it invites believers to continue choosing life by trusting the God whose purposes ultimately lead toward restoration.

This prepares us for the deeper struggles that appear throughout the rest of Scripture.

From the cries of Job to the laments of the prophets and the protests of the psalmists, the Bible repeatedly returns to moments when the moral order of the world appears to fracture.

These moments do not undermine faith.

They reveal how faith persists even when life becomes morally confusing.

And they prepare us for the most profound moment of moral rupture in the biblical story — the crucifixion of Jesus Christ.

But before we arrive there, we must first understand the world the covenant describes.

Deuteronomy 30 invites us to see that world clearly and to hear again the ancient call that still echoes across the life of faith:

"Choose life."

SERMON- THE WORLD GOD INTENDED

Text: Deuteronomy 30

There are moments in life when the world no longer feels morally intelligible.

Most people do not use language like that, of course. They speak more simply, and usually more painfully. They say things like, "I don't understand why this happened." They say, "I tried to do the right thing." They say, "We prayed for years, and this is how it turned out?" Beneath those questions lies something deeper than grief alone. There is sorrow, yes, but there is also disorientation. Something about the world itself no longer seems to fit together the way it once did.

Many of us grow up with a quiet belief that life has a certain moral shape. We assume that goodness should matter. We assume that honesty, loyalty, sacrifice, and faithfulness should lead somewhere good. We teach our children that choices matter, that truth matters, that character matters. We tell them not to lie, not to cheat, not to take what is not theirs, not because these things are merely rules, but because we believe the world is built in such a way that righteousness is life-giving and evil is destructive.

In many ways, Scripture encourages exactly that belief. The Bible does not present the world as morally random. It does not tell us that justice is an illusion or that good and evil are simply human preferences. From the beginning, the biblical story insists that the world is created by a good God, governed by a righteous God, and sustained by a faithful God. Human life is not morally neutral. There is a way of living that leads toward life, and there is a way of living that leads toward death.

That is why Deuteronomy 30 matters so much.

Moses is speaking to Israel at a decisive moment. The wilderness years are nearly over. The people are standing on the edge of the land God promised to their ancestors. Moses knows he will not go with them, so he gathers them and speaks with urgency and tenderness. He reminds them who they are. He reminds them what God has done. He reminds them that covenant life is not arbitrary. It is not a set of meaningless religious duties. It is a way of life ordered toward blessing.

Then he says, "I have set before you life and death, blessing and curse. Therefore choose life" (verse 19).

That sentence is more than a command. It is a revelation of the world God intended.

Moses is not merely saying, "Please behave." He is saying, "This is how reality is meant to work under the rule of God." Life and blessing belong together. Death and destruction belong together. Faithfulness is not disconnected from flourishing. Obedience is not disconnected from life. The covenant is not a random collection of regulations. It is an invitation to live in harmony with the moral order built into creation by the character of God himself.

That means the command to choose life is not simply religious language. It is profoundly human language. It speaks to the deepest structure of existence. Because God is just, justice matters. Because God is faithful, faithfulness matters. Because God is good, goodness matters. The world was not made to reward cruelty, deceit, violence, and greed. It was made for truth, mercy, righteousness, and love.

This is why something in us resonates so deeply when we hear Moses say, "Choose life." Even before we analyze the passage, something inside us says, "Yes, that is how the world ought to be." We want to believe that integrity is not wasted, that kindness is not foolish, that righteousness is not meaningless. We want to believe that the world is more than chaos and that our choices are more than survival strategies.

And according to Scripture, that desire is not naïve. It is an echo of creation.

The world God intended is a world where life makes moral sense.

That does not mean life is easy. It does not mean the covenant erases struggle, labor, risk, or sorrow. But it does mean that creation has a moral grain to it. It means human beings flourish when they live in alignment with the character of God. It means justice is not accidental to the universe. It is woven into its purpose.

When Moses tells Israel to choose life, he is inviting them to live with that grain rather than against it. He is saying, in effect, "Do not build your life against reality. Do not embrace the very things that destroy you. Walk in the ways of the Lord, because those ways are not merely commanded; they are life-giving."

This is one of the reasons sin is so destructive in the Bible. Sin is not merely breaking rules. It is violating the moral fabric of the world. It is moving against the grain of creation. When greed replaces generosity, when violence replaces mercy, when exploitation replaces justice, human beings are not simply becoming less religious. They are becoming less alive. They are choosing death because they are turning away from the God in whom life consists.

So Deuteronomy 30 gives us a world that makes sense. It gives us a world in which blessing and obedience belong together, where covenant faithfulness leads toward life. That is the world God intended.

But of course, that is not always the world we experience.

That is where the pain begins.

People come into church carrying stories that do not seem to fit the world Moses describes. They have tried to choose life. They have tried to be faithful. They have tried to honor God, to love their families, to serve others, to do what is right. And yet the outcome they are living with does not feel like blessing. It feels like loss. It feels like confusion. It feels like injustice. It feels like a fracture between what they were taught to expect and what they now endure.

A faithful husband dies too young, leaving behind a wife who prayed every day for healing. A mother who poured herself into her children watches one of them disappear into addiction or estrangement. A person who has spent years serving the church quietly receives a diagnosis that changes everything in a single afternoon. A family who tried to live honestly and generously finds itself buried in sorrow while those who manipulate and exploit seem to thrive without consequence.

In moments like these, people are not merely asking, "Why am I suffering?" They are asking, "How can the world work this way if God is just?"

That is a different kind of question. It is not only a cry of pain; it is a cry of moral disorientation. It is the experience of discovering that reality no longer feels coherent.

And if we are not careful, Christians can respond too quickly. We rush to reassure. We say God has a plan. We say everything happens for a reason. We say suffering builds character. Those statements may contain truth in the right setting, but they can also miss the deeper wound. Sometimes the person before us is not asking for a theory of providence. Sometimes they are asking whether the world still has moral meaning at all.

This is why Deuteronomy 30 is such an important place to begin. Before Scripture teaches us how to lament the fracture, it first shows us what wholeness looks like. Before the Bible speaks from the ruins, it tells us what the house was meant to be. Before the prophets protest, before Job cries out, before the psalmists ask "How long?", the covenant shows us the world God intended.

And what God intended was life.

That matters because Christian faith is not built on resignation. The Bible does not teach us to shrug at evil and call it normal. It does not ask us to accept corruption, exploitation, betrayal, and death as if these things belong naturally to creation. No, Scripture teaches us to recognize them as violations of the order God intended. They feel wrong because, in the deepest sense, they are wrong. They contradict the world as God made it to be.

That is why the language of lament exists in the Bible at all. The psalmists protest because they know the world should be more just than it is. The prophets rage because they know society should reflect the righteousness of God. Job refuses simplistic explanations because he knows his suffering does not fit the moral formulas his friends keep repeating.

All of them are standing, in one way or another, in the light of Deuteronomy 30.

They know life is supposed to make sense under God.

And because they know that, the rupture is unbearable.

The same is true for us. Our pain is often intensified not only by what happened, but by the fact that it should not have happened this way. We know enough about the goodness of God to expect more from the world than what sin and death now give us. We know enough about justice to be wounded when justice fails. We know enough about love to grieve the cruelty that distorts it. We know enough about life to feel the obscenity of death.

Deuteronomy 30 therefore does not solve the problem of suffering, but it tells us why suffering feels like such a deep contradiction. It is because the world was not created for death. It was created for life. It was not created for curse. It was created for blessing. It was not created for moral chaos. It was created to reflect the character of God.

That is why Moses' words remain so powerful. "Choose life" is not only an ancient covenant exhortation. It is the heartbeat of God's intention for humanity. It is the Creator speaking to creatures and saying, "Live in the world as it was meant to be lived. Do not surrender yourselves to what destroys you. Do not call darkness light. Do not baptize death as wisdom. Choose life."

Yet even that command must be heard carefully. If we read it simplistically, we may imagine that it promises immediate prosperity to every faithful person in every circumstance. But the broader witness of Scripture will not let us stop there. The rest of the Bible shows us that in a fallen world, people can choose life and still suffer. They can love God and still weep. They can obey and still be wounded. The covenant reveals the world God intended, but history reveals how deeply that world has been marred.

And still the command remains: choose life.

Not because life is always easy. Not because faithfulness guarantees immediate relief. Not because the righteous never suffer. But because life is still the will of God for his creation. Because blessing is still truer than curse. Because justice is still more ultimate than injustice. Because the Creator has not abandoned the moral meaning of the world even when that meaning is obscured by sin and sorrow.

In fact, the entire biblical story moves toward the restoration of that moral order. What Deuteronomy announces, the gospel ultimately fulfills. The life that Israel was commanded to choose becomes, in the New Testament, a person to trust. Jesus Christ does not merely tell us to choose life. He declares, "I am the life." In him, the world God intended begins to reappear in the middle of the broken world we actually inhabit.

When Jesus heals the sick, welcomes the outcast, confronts hypocrisy, forgives sinners, and raises the dead, he is not performing random acts of compassion. He is revealing the order of the kingdom. He is showing us what the world looks like when the reign of God is made visible. He is restoring, in signs and wonders, the world that Moses described.

And then, at the cross, the deepest contradiction appears. The one who perfectly embodied the life of God is condemned by the powers of death. The righteous one suffers. The obedient Son is crucified. If anyone ever seemed entitled to the blessings of covenant life, it was Jesus. Yet he is rejected, mocked, and executed.

Which means that even the world God intended must now be understood through the mystery of a broken creation.

But the resurrection declares that the moral order of God has not been defeated. The resurrection is God's vindication of life over death, blessing over curse, righteousness over injustice. It is the announcement that the world Moses described is not a fantasy. It is the future God is bringing to completion.

That is why Christians continue to choose life even in a world that often feels morally fractured. We choose life not because life is always immediately rewarded, but because we know where the story is going. We choose justice because justice belongs to God. We choose mercy because mercy reflects his heart. We choose faithfulness because faithfulness is not wasted, even when it is costly.

Every act of obedience becomes, in that sense, a witness to the world God intended and the world God is restoring. Every refusal of bitterness, every act of generosity, every commitment to truth, every labor for justice, every choice to remain faithful in sorrow is a way of saying, "I still believe life is stronger than death because God is stronger than death."

So when Moses says, "I have set before you life and death, blessing and curse. Therefore choose life," he is not speaking only to Israel on the edge of the promised land. He is speaking to everyone who stands at the intersection of covenant hope and lived confusion. He is speaking to those who know the world is broken but still want to live toward the goodness of God. He is speaking to those who have suffered enough to know that the world often does not make sense, yet still believe that God has not surrendered it to chaos.

And perhaps that is where some of us are today.

Perhaps you have chosen life and still found yourself in grief. Perhaps you have tried to be faithful and still discovered how much of the world feels disordered. Perhaps you are not asking whether God exists, but whether the world still bears the meaning you once believed it had.

If so, hear this clearly: the Bible does not mock that question. It begins by affirming that your intuition was right. The world was meant for life. Goodness does matter. Justice does matter. Faithfulness does matter. Your grief over the brokenness of the world is not evidence that you expected too much from God. It may be evidence that you have seen, however dimly, the world he intended.

And because that world is the one God intends, it is also the one he is restoring.

So choose life. Choose it when the path is clear, and choose it when the path is clouded. Choose it when blessing seems near, and choose it when the world feels morally confusing. Choose it not because you can always see how the promise will unfold, but because the God who gave the promise remains faithful.

Choose life because the Creator has not changed. Choose life because the kingdom is still coming. Choose life because Christ is risen. Choose life because the future belongs not to chaos, not to injustice, not to death, but to the God whose purpose from the beginning has been blessing, life, and peace.

That is the world God intended.

And by his grace, it is the world he will yet bring to fullness.

Chapter 2

When Faith Faces the Unthinkable

Text: Genesis 22

OPENING PASTORAL SCENARIO

Every pastor eventually sits with someone whose faith has collided with an event that seems impossible to understand.

These conversations rarely begin dramatically. More often they surface quietly after worship or during a pastoral visit. A person who has been part of the church for years begins describing something that has shaken their understanding of God.

At first they simply recount what happened—the diagnosis, the loss, the sudden tragedy that changed life in a moment. Gradually the deeper question begins to emerge.

"I don't understand why God would ask this of me."

Sometimes the words are different.

"Why would God allow this?"
"Why would this happen to my family?"
"I thought I was trying to follow God."

What makes these moments so difficult is not only the suffering itself. Human beings have endured hardship throughout history, and believers have often faced pain with remarkable courage.

The deeper struggle is the sense that the suffering does not fit the way the person has understood their relationship with God.

They believed their lives were oriented toward faithfulness. They tried to follow God's leading. They trusted that obedience placed them within the care of a good and faithful God.

Then something happens that makes the world feel morally disorienting.

The person begins to wonder whether the story they believed about God and the world still makes sense.

This is one of the most difficult pastoral moments a preacher encounters.

The question is not simply about suffering. It is about the nature of faith itself.

What happens when obedience leads into something incomprehensible?

What happens when the path of faith seems to contradict everything we believed about the goodness of God?

Moments like these reveal a particular kind of spiritual crisis.

The person is not abandoning faith. In many cases the crisis emerges precisely because they have taken faith seriously. They trusted that following God would place their lives within the wisdom and goodness of God's purposes.

Now that trust feels strained.

Something has happened that makes the world feel morally confusing. The person struggles to understand how the God they love could allow—or even require—what they are facing.

Pastors often feel pressure in these moments to provide answers. We want to reassure people that God remains good and that their suffering somehow fits within a larger purpose.

But explanations can arrive too quickly.

Someone standing inside profound confusion does not always need an immediate answer. Often they need permission to acknowledge that what they are experiencing feels deeply unsettling.

The Bible itself recognizes this kind of moment.

One of the most disturbing stories in Scripture begins with a command that appears to shatter the expectations of the believer who receives it.

The story is found in Genesis 22.

If the covenant describes a world ordered toward life, Genesis 22 introduces a moment when that vision appears to break.

Abraham, the man who trusted God's promises, receives a command that seems to contradict the very promise that defined his faith.

The story therefore confronts us with a deeply unsettling question: what happens when obedience to God leads into something that feels morally incomprehensible?

For many readers this passage is one of the most difficult texts in the entire Bible. God commands Abraham—the man who has trusted God's promises for decades—to take his son Isaac to a mountain and offer him as a sacrifice.

The shock of the command is impossible to ignore.

Isaac is not simply Abraham's child. He is the child of promise, the son through whom God has pledged to build the future. Isaac represents the fulfillment of everything Abraham has trusted God to accomplish.

Now God appears to ask Abraham to give him up.

For modern readers the command feels morally troubling. It raises questions that resist easy answers.

Why would God ask such a thing?

How could Abraham reconcile this command with everything he believed about the goodness of God?

The story confronts us with a moment when faith itself seems to lead into profound confusion.

Abraham has spent his life learning to trust God. He left his homeland because God called him. He followed God's leading through years of uncertainty. He waited patiently for the promise of a child.

Again and again his story has demonstrated that faith means trusting God's word even when the future is unclear.

Yet Genesis 22 presents Abraham with a situation unlike anything he has faced before.

This time the command appears to contradict the very promise that defined his faith.

Isaac is the child through whom God promised to bless the nations. He represents the future God has pledged to create.

Now God tells Abraham to place that promise on the altar.

The tension is overwhelming.

The command appears to undermine everything Abraham believes about the character and purposes of God. Faithfulness now leads directly into a situation that feels impossible to understand.

It is difficult to imagine what Abraham felt as he began the journey to the mountain.

The text itself is strikingly restrained. It does not describe Abraham's emotions. Instead it simply tells us that he rises early in the morning and begins the journey.

Yet the silence of the narrative intensifies the weight of the moment.

Every step toward the mountain carries a question that remains unresolved.

How can obedience to God require something that appears morally unbearable?

This is the kind of question many believers eventually face.

The circumstances differ, but the experience is familiar. Someone who has tried to live faithfully finds themselves standing inside a moment that does not make sense.

The God they trust appears to be leading them into something they cannot reconcile with the goodness they believe defines God's character.

Genesis 22 gives voice to this experience.

The story does not begin by explaining the mystery. Instead it invites the reader to stand beside Abraham as he confronts a command that challenges everything he thought he understood.

For pastors this passage opens a profound opportunity for preaching.

Rather than avoiding the tension in the story, we can recognize that the text itself explores a moment when faith encounters something that feels morally incomprehensible.

Genesis 22 shows us what faith looks like when obedience leads into territory where the meaning of events suddenly becomes uncertain.

THE PASSAGE AS WE USUALLY PREACH IT

Genesis 22 is one of the most well-known stories in the Old Testament, and for generations it has shaped sermons about faith and obedience.

Most readers remember the basic outline of the story. God calls Abraham and instructs him to take his son Isaac to a mountain and offer him as a sacrifice. Abraham obeys, travels to the mountain, builds the altar, and raises the knife. At the final moment God intervenes, stopping the sacrifice and providing a ram instead.

In many sermons the focus falls on Abraham's obedience.

Abraham becomes the supreme example of faith. Faced with a command he does not understand, he trusts God completely. He does not argue, demand an explanation, or turn away from the command. Instead, he obeys.

Within this interpretation the story becomes a powerful illustration of surrender. True faith means trusting God even when obedience is difficult and the future is uncertain.

This emphasis highlights an important biblical truth. The life of faith does involve trust and surrender. Believers are called to follow God even when the path forward is unclear and obedience requires sacrifice.

In this sense Genesis 22 becomes a story about the depth of Abraham's trust.

Abraham continues toward the mountain because he believes God remains faithful even when the command feels impossible to understand.

Many sermons also emphasize the moment when God intervenes.

Just as Abraham prepares to sacrifice Isaac, an angel calls from heaven and stops him. A ram appears in the thicket and becomes the substitute sacrifice. The story concludes with a renewed affirmation of God's promise that Abraham's descendants will bless the nations.

Within this interpretation the passage becomes a reassuring message about God's provision.

God tests Abraham's faith, but ultimately God provides what is needed.

There is genuine truth in this interpretation. The story does reveal Abraham's remarkable trust, and the provision of the ram does point to the faithfulness of God.

Yet when the passage is preached only in this way, something essential in the narrative can be overlooked.

The moral shock of the command itself is often softened or passed over too quickly.

The story begins with words that should stop the reader in their tracks:

"Take your son, your only son Isaac, whom you love… and offer him there as a burnt offering" (Gen 22:2).

The language is deliberately intense. Every phrase reminds the reader what Isaac means to Abraham.

Your son.
Your only son.
The one you love.

The command is not simply difficult. It appears to contradict everything the reader has learned about God's promise.

Isaac represents the future God has sworn to create.

Now the command appears to destroy that future.

If we move too quickly past this tension, we miss something essential about the story.

Genesis 22 is not only about obedience.

It is about the moment when obedience appears to collide with the very promises of God.

The command places Abraham in a situation where the meaning of faith itself becomes uncertain.

Everything Abraham believes about God tells him that God is faithful and trustworthy.

Yet the command he has received seems to undermine the promise that has guided his entire life.

The tension is profound.

If Abraham obeys the command, the promise appears to die with Isaac.

If he refuses, he disobeys the God he has trusted for decades.

This is what makes the story so unsettling.

Abraham is not simply being asked to surrender something valuable. He is being asked to act in a way that seems to contradict the foundation of his faith.

The narrative therefore invites the reader to sit inside the tension before the resolution arrives.

Genesis 22 becomes more than an illustration of obedience.

It becomes a story about what happens when faith itself encounters the unthinkable.

THE MORAL INJURY QUESTION

At this point in the story the preacher must pause and ask an uncomfortable question.

Where does the moral world appear to break in this passage?

When we read Genesis 22 carefully, the tension is not merely emotional. It is deeply theological.

Abraham is not simply facing a difficult decision. He is confronting a command that appears to contradict everything he has learned about God.

For decades Abraham has lived within a story defined by promise.

God called him to leave his homeland and journey toward a future he could not yet see. God promised that his descendants would become a great nation and that through them the world would be blessed.

At the center of that promise stands Isaac.

Isaac is not only Abraham's beloved son. He is the embodiment of God's covenant promise.

Years earlier God made it unmistakably clear that the future of the covenant would come through this child.

Isaac is the miracle that confirmed God's faithfulness.

Abraham and Sarah waited years for him. They endured uncertainty and disappointment. When Isaac was finally born, the promise seemed secure.

Everything Abraham believed about God was tied to that promise.

Now Genesis 22 introduces a command that threatens to dismantle it.

"Take your son, your only son Isaac, whom you love… and offer him there as a burnt offering."

The words are stark.

The God who gave the promise now appears to demand its destruction.

For Abraham this moment must have felt like the collapse of the moral world he had trusted.

Until now his journey with God had always moved in the direction of life.

Genesis 22 suddenly reverses that direction.

The command points toward death.

This is what creates the crisis within the story.

Abraham must reconcile two realities that seem impossible to hold together.

He believes God is faithful.

Yet the command he has received appears to undermine that faithfulness.

If Isaac dies, the promise dies with him.

The world Abraham trusted suddenly feels unstable.

This is the kind of experience we now describe as moral injury.

The expectations that once made life coherent suddenly collapse.

Something similar is happening within Abraham's story.

For years he has interpreted his life through the conviction that God's promises lead toward life.

Genesis 22 places that conviction under immense pressure.

The reader is therefore forced to confront a disturbing possibility.

What if obedience to God leads into something that feels morally incomprehensible?

Genesis 22 does not immediately resolve that question.

Instead it invites the reader to remain inside the tension.

WHAT THE MORAL INJURY LENS REVEALS

Once we recognize the rupture within Genesis 22, the story begins to open in ways that many sermons never fully explore.

The passage is often treated primarily as a lesson about obedience. Abraham trusts God completely, and the reader is encouraged to imitate that trust. While this interpretation contains truth, it does not fully account for the emotional and theological tension that dominates the narrative.

The story is not only about obedience. It is about faith confronted with something that appears morally unbearable.

The command Abraham receives is not merely difficult. It threatens the very promise that has defined his relationship with God.

The God who promised life now appears to command death.

The God who created the future through Isaac now seems to demand that future be placed on an altar.

Seen this way, Abraham's experience reflects something profoundly human. He is not simply being asked to surrender something valuable. He is facing a moment when the moral coherence of his world has been shattered.

Everything Abraham believed about God's promise appears to collapse.

For many believers, moments like this feel frighteningly familiar.

People often enter the life of faith believing that the world possesses a moral order grounded in the character of God. They trust that God is good, that God's purposes lead toward life, and that obedience places them within that goodness.

Then something happens that seems impossible to reconcile with that belief.

A child dies.
A marriage collapses.
A diagnosis changes everything.

Suddenly the vision through which life once made sense begins to feel unstable.

The believer may still trust God, but they struggle to understand how the events unfolding in their life can fit within the goodness of God.

Genesis 22 gives voice to that experience.

The story shows what faith looks like when obedience leads into a situation that appears morally incomprehensible.

Abraham does not receive an explanation. The text never records God telling him why this command has been given. He is simply told to go to the mountain.

This silence is significant.

Many assume that faith always provides clarity. Yet the story of Abraham suggests that faith sometimes involves continuing forward even when clarity is absent.

Abraham walks toward the mountain carrying a promise that now feels deeply uncertain.

Here the moral injury lens reveals something important about the nature of faith.

Faith is not simply confidence that everything will make sense.

Faith is the willingness to remain in relationship with God even when the meaning of events becomes difficult to understand.

Abraham does not stop trusting God, but his trust now exists within profound tension. He cannot reconcile the command with the promise, yet he continues walking.

For pastors, recognizing this dimension of the story is crucial.

Many believers quietly assume that their confusion disqualifies them from faith. When life stops making sense, they begin to wonder whether their questions reveal weakness or spiritual failure.

Genesis 22 challenges that assumption.

The story suggests that faith can exist even within moments when the moral coherence of the world appears to collapse.

Abraham does not possess certainty about what will happen on the mountain. He does not understand how the promise of God can survive the command he has received.

Yet he continues walking.

This is not blind obedience that ignores the tension of the moment. It is a form of trust that persists even when understanding fails.

The narrative itself reflects this tension.

As Abraham and Isaac walk together, Isaac finally speaks.

"Father… where is the lamb for the burnt offering?" (verse 7).

It is one of the most haunting questions in Scripture.

Isaac sees the wood.
He sees the fire.
But he does not see the sacrifice.

Abraham's answer expresses both faith and uncertainty.

"God himself will provide the lamb" (verse 8).

The statement reveals hope, but it does not explain how that hope will unfold. Abraham is still walking toward the altar, and from his perspective the outcome remains unknown.

The story forces the reader to remain inside that uncertainty.

Only at the final moment does the resolution arrive.

As Abraham prepares to carry out the command, God intervenes. The voice from heaven stops the sacrifice, and a ram appears in the thicket as a substitute offering.

The promise survives.

Yet the journey to that moment matters.

Genesis 22 does not hide the tension that leads to the resolution. Instead it allows the reader to feel the weight of Abraham's experience before the outcome becomes clear.

This is why the passage speaks so powerfully to believers who feel as though their own lives have entered moments of deep confusion.

The story acknowledges that faith sometimes leads into situations where the future feels uncertain and the meaning of events is difficult to interpret.

Yet it also suggests that God remains present within those moments.

Abraham names the place of the encounter with a remarkable phrase: "The Lord will provide."

The name does not erase the tension Abraham experienced on the mountain. Instead it reflects what he discovered in the midst of it.

Even when the path of faith leads into moments that seem incomprehensible, God has not abandoned the story.

Recognizing this dimension of Genesis 22 changes how the passage speaks to the life of faith.

The story is not merely about extraordinary obedience. It is about what happens when faith confronts something that feels morally impossible.

And once we see that, the passage begins to speak directly to the experiences many believers carry with them into worship each week.

The question then becomes clear.

How should this story be preached to people who are already wrestling with moments when their own world has stopped making sense?

That is the question we turn to next.

HOW THIS CHANGES THE SERMON

Recognizing the rupture within Genesis 22 changes the way this passage can be preached.

Many sermons approach this story primarily as an example of radical obedience. Abraham becomes the model of faith because he trusts God completely, even when the command appears difficult or confusing. The congregation is encouraged to imitate Abraham by surrendering everything to God.

This interpretation highlights an important dimension of faith. Trust and surrender are essential to the life of discipleship.

Yet when the story is preached only this way, it can create distance between the biblical narrative and the lived experience of the congregation.

Most believers are not standing on a mountain with a knife in their hands.

They are sitting in pews carrying questions about events that have already unfolded in their lives.

They have already faced moments when the world they trusted seemed to collapse.

They prayed for healing and watched illness continue.
They trusted God and experienced loss anyway.
They tried to live faithfully and encountered circumstances that felt deeply unfair.

When sermons focus only on Abraham's obedience, listeners may quietly wonder how their own experiences fit within the life of faith.

Some may even assume that their confusion reflects a failure to trust God.

Reading Genesis 22 through the lens of moral injury opens another way of preaching this passage.

Instead of emphasizing obedience alone, the sermon can acknowledge the moment when faith itself encounters something that feels morally incomprehensible.

The story suddenly becomes recognizable.

Abraham's journey toward the mountain reflects an experience many believers know in different forms. It is the experience of continuing to walk with God when the path ahead feels impossible to understand.

The preacher can speak honestly about the tension within the text.

Genesis 22 does not present a simple moral lesson. It places Abraham in a situation where the command of God appears to contradict the promise of God.

The passage allows the congregation to see that even the most faithful believers may encounter moments when the meaning of life feels uncertain.

This recognition changes the tone of the sermon.

Instead of urging the congregation to achieve Abraham's level of obedience, the preacher can acknowledge that faith sometimes leads into seasons where obedience itself feels confusing.

People do not need to pretend those moments are easy.

They do not need to hide the questions that arise when life stops making sense.

Genesis 22 gives them permission to recognize that faith can exist even within the tension of confusion.

This also deepens the pastoral honesty of the sermon.

Rather than offering quick explanations for suffering, the preacher can acknowledge that some moments in the life of faith are genuinely difficult to interpret.

Abraham does not receive an explanation before he begins the journey to the mountain.

He simply hears the command and begins walking.

Many listeners will recognize something of their own experience in that image.

They too have walked through moments when the future felt unclear and the meaning of events was difficult to discern.

The story suggests that faith does not eliminate those moments.

Sometimes faith means continuing the journey even when understanding remains incomplete.

This perspective also strengthens the theological depth of the sermon.

Genesis 22 reveals that God is present even within moments that appear morally confusing.

Abraham does not understand the command he has received, yet the story ultimately shows that God has not abandoned the promise.

The intervention on the mountain does not erase the tension of the journey.

Instead it reveals that God's purposes extend beyond what Abraham could see while he was walking toward the altar.

This truth allows the sermon to move toward hope without ignoring the tension that precedes it.

Preachers do not need to rush to the resolution of the story.

They can allow the congregation to feel the weight of Abraham's journey before the ram appears in the thicket.

In doing so, the sermon becomes more honest about the nature of faith.

Faith is not always the absence of confusion.

Sometimes faith is the willingness to remain in relationship with God even when the meaning of events feels uncertain.

For many listeners this recognition brings relief.

They realize that their questions do not disqualify them from faith. Their confusion does not mean they have failed to trust God.

Instead, their experience places them within the long story of believers who have walked with God through moments that felt impossible to understand.

Genesis 22 becomes a story about faith that continues even when life no longer makes sense.

When the sermon is preached in this way, Abraham's journey no longer feels distant or abstract.

It reflects something deeply human—the experience of trusting God while standing inside a moment that feels morally overwhelming.

And this prepares the congregation for the proclamation that follows.

The sermon that concludes this chapter explores how Genesis 22 can be proclaimed to people who are trying to remain faithful even when the world they trusted has been shaken.

It asks a question that lies at the heart of the life of faith:

What does trust look like when obedience leads into the unthinkable?

SERMON - WHEN FAITH FACES THE UNTHINKABLE

Text: Genesis 22

There are moments in life when faith becomes much harder than we ever imagined it would.

Most people do not begin the life of faith expecting ease, but many do begin it expecting a certain moral clarity. We assume that if we trust God, if we seek to obey him, if we try to walk faithfully, then even the painful parts of life will at least fit within some intelligible pattern. We know there will be sorrow. We know there will be trials. We know discipleship is not the same thing as comfort. But we still tend to believe that the path of obedience will somehow remain recognizable as the path of a good God.

Then something happens that disturbs that expectation.

A diagnosis arrives that prayer did not prevent. A child's life begins to move in a direction no parent would choose. A marriage breaks apart after years of effort and faithfulness. A family that tried to build its life around trust, obedience, and hope finds itself standing in a place of loss, bewilderment, and grief. In those moments, the question is not only, "Why am I suffering?" The deeper question is, "How can this be the path God has allowed? How can the God I trust lead me here?"

That is not simply pain. It is moral confusion. It is the experience of standing inside a moment that feels incompatible with everything you thought you knew about the goodness of God.

That is why Genesis 22 remains one of the most unsettling chapters in all of Scripture. It does not merely tell the story of a difficult test. It tells the story of a faithful man confronted with something that appears impossible to reconcile with the very God he has spent his life trusting.

By the time we arrive at Genesis 22, Abraham has already walked a long road with God. He has left his homeland in obedience to a call he did not fully understand. He has trusted promises that stretched across years of uncertainty. He has waited for God when the future seemed delayed. He has stumbled at times, certainly, but he has kept returning to the God who called him. Over and over again, Abraham's life has been shaped by a single reality: the promise of God.

And at the center of that promise stands Isaac.

Isaac is not just Abraham's beloved son. Isaac is the child of promise. He is the sign that God has kept his word. He is the future Abraham has been waiting for. Through Isaac the covenant is supposed to continue. Through Isaac nations are supposed to be blessed. Through Isaac the impossible goodness of God has finally taken visible form.

And then Genesis 22 opens with words that have troubled readers for centuries:

"Take your son, your only son Isaac, whom you love... and offer him there as a burnt offering."

There are some passages of Scripture that should make us stop and feel the full force of what is being said. This is one of them. The text does not hurry. It lingers over every phrase.

Your son.
Your only son.
Whom you love.

The command is not simply difficult. It seems to strike directly at the heart of the promise itself. The God who gave Abraham this child now appears to ask for that child back. The God who promised life now appears to command death. The God who built a future through Isaac now seems to demand that the future be laid on an altar.

That is what makes this text so unsettling.

Abraham is not merely being asked to surrender something precious. He is being asked to walk into a situation where the command of God appears to contradict the promise of God.

And that is why Genesis 22 matters so much for the life of faith. This chapter is not only about obedience. It is about what faith looks like when obedience itself becomes incomprehensible. It is about what happens when the path of trust leads into something that feels morally unbearable.

There are many believers who know, in one way or another, what that feels like.

They know what it is to try to walk faithfully and still end up in places they cannot make sense of. They know what it is to pray sincerely and still find themselves carrying burdens they do not understand. They know what it is to believe that God is good and still feel deeply troubled by the road on which they now stand.

Genesis 22 gives voice to that experience because it does not rush to explanation. It does not begin by saying, "Here is why God gave the command."

It does not soften the blow with an immediate resolution. It simply tells us what happened.

God spoke. Abraham rose early. He prepared the donkey. He took the wood, the knife, and the fire. Then he began the journey.

The silence of the story is part of its power. We are not told what Abraham said to Sarah. We are not told what passed through his mind as he prepared for the journey. We are not given a window into all the emotions that must have filled his heart. Instead, the narrative simply allows us to watch him walk.

And he walks for three days.

Three days is a long time to carry an unbearable command. Three days is a long time to keep moving while the heart asks questions the mind cannot answer. Three days is a long time to wonder how the God you trust could possibly be asking something like this.

The text forces us to slow down because Abraham himself has no quick way through the crisis. He must live inside it. He must keep walking before he can see any sign of resolution.

Then, as if the tension were not already heavy enough, Isaac speaks.

"Father."

There is pain in that word. Abraham answers, "Here I am, my son." Isaac sees the fire. He sees the wood. But he notices something is missing.

"Where is the lamb for the burnt offering?"

That question sits at the center of the chapter. Isaac does not yet understand what Abraham understands. He sees the elements of sacrifice, but he does not see the offering.

Abraham responds, "God himself will provide the lamb."

Those words are beautiful, but they are also agonizing, because Abraham does not yet know how they will be fulfilled. He speaks trust, but he does not speak from clarity. He confesses hope while still walking toward the altar. His words are not the polished certainty of someone who has solved the mystery. They are the trembling confession of a man who is holding on to God at the edge of moral confusion.

That is where this story becomes deeply pastoral.

Many people assume faith means clarity. They assume faith means being able to explain what God is doing. They assume faith means moving through life with confidence and certainty. But Genesis 22 reveals something different. Faith is not always full understanding. Sometimes faith is what remains when understanding has failed. Sometimes faith is the willingness to keep walking with God even when the moral logic of life has become obscure.

Abraham does not understand how the command and the promise can both be true. He cannot reconcile them. He cannot fit them into a neat theological framework. Yet he keeps walking.

That matters because there are many believers who quietly fear that their confusion means their faith is failing. They imagine that if they were stronger, holier, more mature, they would not feel so unsettled by what they are facing. But Abraham's story tells a different truth. The father of faith is not presented here as a man for whom everything is simple. He is presented as a man who trusts God while walking into something he cannot possibly understand.

The life of faith, then, does not always protect us from confusion. Sometimes it leads us into places where confusion becomes the very context in which trust must survive.

That does not make the confusion holy in itself. Genesis 22 does not romanticize anguish. It does not suggest that pain is somehow automatically beautiful. But it does show us that confusion does not disqualify a person from faith. The person who trembles may still be faithful. The person who cannot yet make sense of the road may still be walking with God.

And that is important, because there are moments in life when the only honest thing a believer can say is, "I do not understand this." There are moments when obedience does not feel inspiring. It feels terrifying. There are moments when faith does not look like triumph. It looks like putting one foot in front of another because there is nowhere else to go.

Genesis 22 refuses to shame that kind of faith.

Instead, it honors it.

Of course, this raises another question, and it is one we cannot avoid. What kind of God is revealed in this story?

We cannot stop with Abraham's obedience. We also have to ask what Abraham discovers about God on the mountain.

The answer comes only at the final moment. Abraham builds the altar. He arranges the wood. He binds Isaac. He stretches out his hand and takes the knife. And then the voice of the Lord breaks in.

"Abraham, Abraham" (verse 11).

The command is stopped. The sacrifice is not carried out. A ram appears in the thicket and becomes the substitute.

And suddenly we see something Abraham could not have seen while he was still climbing.

God had not abandoned the promise.

The God who allowed Abraham to walk into the crisis is also the God who meets him within it. The God who permitted the tension is also the God who provides in the tension. The God who seemed hidden on the journey is revealed at the altar as the God who does not let the story end in death.

That does not erase the terror of the road Abraham walked. It does not make the mountain easy. But it does reveal something decisive about God.

The mountain was never outside God's faithfulness.

Abraham could not see that at the beginning. He could not see the ram from the bottom of the hill. He could not see provision while carrying the knife. He could not see resolution while hearing only the command. But the provision was already there in the purpose of God, waiting for the appointed moment.

That is why Abraham names the place, "The Lord will provide" (verse 14).

That name is not sentimental. It is hard won. It is spoken by someone who has walked through fear and confusion and discovered, at the edge of the unthinkable, that God has not abandoned the promise.

There are believers who can testify to something similar. They may still not understand the road they were made to walk. They may never be able to explain why the mountain was necessary. But they can say, with deep humility and trembling honesty, "I found that God did not leave me there." They may not be able to solve the mystery, but they know they were not forsaken inside it.

And that is where Genesis 22 begins to point beyond itself.

Because the deepest truth of this story is not simply that Abraham trusted or that God provided a ram. The deepest truth is that this mountain foreshadows another mountain, another beloved son, another act of surrender, and another revelation of divine provision.

Christians have long seen that Genesis 22 points forward. Not in a simple one-to-one way, but in a profound redemptive way. On another hill, another beloved Son would carry wood toward the place of sacrifice. On another day, a Father would not spare his Son. On another altar, the provision would not be a ram caught in a thicket, but the Son of God himself given for the life of the world.

At the cross, the unthinkable happens in an even deeper way than in Genesis 22.

There, too, the moral logic of the world seems to collapse. The innocent one suffers. The faithful one is condemned. The Son who perfectly embodies the will of the Father is rejected by the powers of the world. If anyone ever appeared to deserve blessing, it was Jesus. And yet Jesus goes to the cross.

Which means that if you want to know whether God understands what it means for faith to face the unthinkable, the answer is not theoretical. The answer is the cross.

God does not remain distant from the mountains his people climb. In Jesus Christ, God enters the place of anguish himself. He steps into the place where obedience, suffering, trust, and grief meet. He does not explain away pain from a safe distance. He bears it.

And then, in the resurrection, God declares that the final meaning of the story is not death but life.

The resurrection matters here because without it, the cross would simply be another example of moral collapse. But in raising Jesus from the dead, God reveals that his purposes are deeper than the apparent triumph of suffering and loss. He reveals that what seems like the victory of death is not the end of the story.

That is why Christians do not read Genesis 22 as people who are still wondering whether God is trustworthy. We read it as people who have seen the trustworthiness of God revealed in Christ crucified and risen. We read it knowing that the God Abraham trusted has now shown his heart in Jesus. We read it knowing that divine provision does not always appear early, but it does appear. We read it knowing that God's faithfulness may be hidden for a time, but it is never absent.

So what does this mean for us now?

It means, first, that the life of faith may indeed lead into places we never would have chosen. Obedience is not a contract guaranteeing ease. Following God does not mean we will always understand the road before us. There are seasons when trust must endure without clarity.

It means, second, that confusion is not the same thing as unbelief. The believer who struggles to reconcile experience with promise is not therefore outside the life of faith. Sometimes the most faithful people are the ones who keep walking while their questions remain unanswered.

It means, third, that God's provision often cannot be seen at the beginning of the journey. Abraham did not begin with the ram already in his hands. He walked without seeing how God would act. Many believers know that experience. They do not yet see the answer, the healing, the provision, or the resolution. They are still on the road. Genesis 22 does not belittle that. It dignifies it.

It means, finally, that the deepest answer to the unthinkable is not a neat explanation but the character of God himself. Abraham could not fully understand the command, but he learned that God remained faithful. Christians can say even more because we have seen that faithfulness in Jesus Christ. We know that God's hiddenness is not cruelty. We know that his silence is not abandonment. We know that the God who calls his people to trust is the God who has already given himself for them.

So if you are standing in a place where the moral logic of life feels uncertain, hear this clearly: you are not alone there. Abraham has stood there. The prophets have stood there. The psalmists have stood there. The disciples stood there at the cross. And above all, Christ has entered that place and made it his own.

You may not understand the mountain you are climbing. You may not yet be able to reconcile what you are facing with the promise you once thought was clear. You may still be asking where the lamb is, where the answer is, where the provision is, where God is.

Genesis 22 does not ask you to pretend those questions are not real.

But it does tell you this: the God who seemed hidden on the road was already present in the story. The God who felt silent on the ascent was still the God who would provide. The God who allowed Abraham to walk into the unthinkable was not a God of abandonment but a God of hidden faithfulness.

And because of Jesus Christ, we now know that hidden faithfulness more clearly than Abraham ever did.

So keep walking.

Keep praying, even if your prayers sound more like cries than conclusions. Keep trusting, even if your trust trembles. Keep placing one foot in front of the other, not because you understand everything, but because the God who met Abraham on the mountain has met the world in Christ and has not let death have the final word.

That is what faith looks like when it faces the unthinkable. It is not polished certainty. It is not easy calm. It is the costly, trembling refusal to let go of God when everything else has become hard to understand.

And it is sustained by this hope: the Lord will provide.

He may not provide on our timeline, and he may not provide in the form we expected. But the mountain will not be beyond his reach. The promise will not finally fail. The story will not end with the knife.

The God of Abraham is still the God of resurrection. And for those who walk by faith, even through the unthinkable, that is enough to keep going.

Chapter 3

When Justice Appears Delayed

Text: Habakkuk 1–2

OPENING PASTORAL SCENARIO: WHEN EVIL SEEMS TO WIN

Every pastor eventually hears a version of the same troubling question.

It may come from a congregant sitting across the desk in a quiet office. The person has been watching the news, reading headlines, and trying to reconcile what they see with what they believe about God. After a few moments of hesitation they finally say something like this:

"Why do the worst people seem to get away with everything?"

Sometimes the question arises after a painful situation in the community. A business owner cheats employees and grows wealthier. A public figure abuses power and appears untouchable. Violence erupts in a city, yet justice moves slowly or not at all. In these moments people are not simply upset about injustice. Something deeper has been disturbed. The world no longer appears to operate according to the moral order they believed governed it.

Many believers grow up trusting that God governs the world with justice. Scripture repeatedly affirms that God cares about righteousness and opposes evil. The prophets speak passionately about justice flowing like a river and righteousness like a mighty stream. The Psalms declare that the Lord defends the oppressed and brings down the wicked. Yet when people look at the world around them, those assurances can feel painfully distant. Evil seems to flourish, corruption appears to go unchecked, and the righteous often suffer quietly while the wicked prosper loudly.

In moments like these believers sometimes begin to wrestle with a disturbing thought: if God truly governs the world with justice, why does injustice seem to win so often?

Pastors know how delicate that moment can be. The instinct is often to move quickly toward reassurance. We remind people that God is still in control and assure them that justice will eventually prevail. Those truths are important and deeply biblical. Yet Scripture itself does something surprising with this question. Instead of silencing it, the Bible gives it a voice.

One of the clearest examples appears in the book of the prophet Habakkuk. Habakkuk lives in a time when violence, corruption, and injustice dominate the land. As the prophet surveys the world around him, he cannot reconcile what he sees with what he believes about God. So Habakkuk does something bold: he brings his complaint directly to God.

The book opens with a protest that is both honest and unsettling:

"How long, O Lord, must I call for help, but you do not listen?" (Hab 1:2).

Habakkuk is not speaking about God to others. He is speaking directly to God. The prophet looks at the world and sees violence, injustice, and corruption spreading across the land. What troubles him most is not simply that evil exists but that God appears to be doing nothing about it. He continues with a question that sounds almost accusatory:

"Why do you make me look at injustice? Why do you tolerate wrongdoing?" (verse 3).

These words are startling in their directness. Habakkuk is not offering a polite prayer but raising a moral protest. The world, as he sees it, is not behaving the way a just world should behave. Violence is everywhere, justice seems paralyzed, and the wicked surround the righteous. In Habakkuk's experience the order that should reflect God's justice no longer appears reliable.

This moment marks an important shift in the unfolding story of Scripture. In the previous chapter we saw Abraham confronted with a command that seemed to contradict the promise of God. Abraham's crisis was deeply personal. His faith was tested in a moment that defied moral understanding. In Habakkuk the crisis expands beyond one individual. The prophet looks at society itself and sees injustice spreading unchecked.

For many believers today, Habakkuk's words feel surprisingly familiar. People see corruption in public life, watch violence unfold in their communities, and observe systems that reward greed while punishing integrity. They hear the language of justice spoken loudly but see little evidence that justice is actually being done. In those moments the ancient question rises again: How long, O Lord?

This question is not merely emotional. It is theological. Habakkuk believes something about God that makes the situation unbearable. He believes that God is just, that God cares about righteousness, and that the world should reflect the character of its Creator. When reality seems to contradict that belief, the tension becomes difficult to ignore.

The book of Habakkuk therefore introduces a crucial dimension of the biblical story. Faith does not always experience the world as morally coherent. Sometimes believers look at reality and see a troubling gap between what they believe about God and what they see happening around them. That gap can feel deeply unsettling.

Yet the Bible does not hide from this tension. Instead it preserves the voice of a prophet who dared to bring his protest directly before God. Habakkuk's prayer reveals that faithful people sometimes wrestle honestly with the apparent delay of divine justice. The prophet does not abandon his faith, but neither does he pretend that everything makes sense.

Violence is everywhere, justice is failing, and God appears silent.

For pastors and congregations today, Habakkuk offers something deeply important: permission. Permission to acknowledge that the world sometimes looks profoundly unjust. Permission to admit that believers sometimes struggle to understand why evil seems to flourish. Permission to bring those questions directly to God.

This honesty is not a sign of weak faith. In the biblical tradition it is often the beginning of deeper faith.

The story of Habakkuk invites us into the next stage of the biblical journey through moral rupture. After Abraham's personal crisis, Scripture now introduces the broader question of injustice within the world itself. If God governs the world with justice, why does injustice appear to prevail?

This question echoes throughout the rest of the biblical narrative. It appears in the anguished protests of Job, shapes the language of lament in the Psalms, and deepens in the cries of the exiled community as Jerusalem lies in ruins. Ultimately it reaches its most dramatic expression at the cross, where the innocent Son of God suffers at the hands of an unjust world.

But before we arrive there, we must listen carefully to the voice of Habakkuk. The prophet stands at the edge of a moral crisis and refuses to look away. He dares to speak honestly about what he sees, forcing us to confront a question believers have asked for centuries: What does faith look like when evil seems to win?

THE PASSAGE AS WE USUALLY PREACH IT

When pastors preach from Habakkuk, the sermon most often centers on one familiar line: "The righteous shall live by faith" (Hab 2:4). This phrase later becomes central to New Testament theology. The apostle Paul quotes it in Romans and Galatians when explaining justification, and the author of Hebrews draws on the same verse when encouraging perseverance.

Because of this, sermons on Habakkuk frequently emphasize faith in difficult circumstances. Life can be confusing. We do not always understand what God is doing. Yet faithful people trust God even when the outcome is unclear. There is genuine truth in this message. Faith does involve trusting God when life becomes difficult, and Habakkuk himself eventually declares that even if the fields produce no food and the flocks disappear from the stalls, he will still rejoice in the Lord.

Yet when sermons move too quickly to that conclusion, something important in the text can be lost.

The book of Habakkuk does not begin with calm faith. It begins with protest. The prophet opens the book with a raw complaint directed toward God. He is not quietly reflecting on the mysteries of providence but wrestling with the apparent failure of justice in the world around him. His cry—"How long, O Lord?"—does not sound like the voice of someone who has already resolved his theological questions.

Violence fills the land, injustice spreads through society, and God appears silent.

Many sermons move past this opening protest quickly, mentioning Habakkuk's complaint only briefly before turning to the later verses that emphasize trust. But doing so skips over the central struggle of the book. Habakkuk is not simply learning to trust God in the abstract. He is confronting a crisis in which the world no longer seems to reflect the justice of God.

This tension lies at the heart of the passage. If sermons focus only on the call to "live by faith," the deeper question raised by Habakkuk can disappear. Why does injustice appear to win?

This question is not merely philosophical. It is deeply pastoral. People in the pews often wrestle with it more than preachers realize. They see corruption in public life, experience unfair treatment in workplaces, and watch destructive people thrive while faithful people struggle. When those realities collide with the belief that God governs the world with justice, confusion naturally follows.

Many believers carry that confusion quietly because they assume that expressing such questions might sound irreverent. Yet Scripture itself gives voice to these questions repeatedly. The prophets ask them, the psalmists sing them, Job shouts them, and Habakkuk brings them directly before God.

When sermons avoid this tension, congregations miss the profound honesty of the biblical text. Habakkuk teaches us that faithful people sometimes wrestle openly with the apparent delay of divine justice. The prophet refuses to pretend that everything makes sense. Instead he brings his confusion before God and waits for an answer.

THE MORAL INJURY QUESTION: WHERE DOES THE MORAL WORLD BREAK?

At this point the preacher must ask a diagnostic question central to this book: where does the moral world appear to break in this passage?

Habakkuk believes that God is just and that the world should reflect that justice. Yet when he looks around him he sees something entirely different. Violence spreads across the land, the law becomes ineffective, the wicked surround the righteous, and justice itself appears distorted.

The prophet therefore experiences a profound contradiction. The world he observes does not match the world he believes God intends.

This is precisely the kind of rupture modern scholars describe as moral injury. Moral injury occurs when deeply held moral expectations are violated by reality. Something happens that contradicts the way the world is supposed to work. The result is not merely sadness or disappointment but a deeper sense that the meaning of events has been shaken.

Habakkuk expected a world where justice prevailed. Instead he sees injustice flourishing. His protest therefore reveals a moment when the moral coherence of the world appears to break.

Yet the protest itself reveals something important.

Habakkuk asks these questions because he believes God is just. If he did not believe in divine justice, he would have no reason to protest. His complaint grows out of faith.

This is one of the most important insights for preachers to recognize. In Scripture protest is not the opposite of faith. Often it is faith wounded by the apparent failure of the world to reflect God's justice.

Habakkuk does not abandon God. He brings his confusion directly to God and then waits. The prophet climbs the watchtower and waits for God's response. This posture reveals something profound about biblical faith. Faith does not require believers to suppress their confusion. It invites them to bring their deepest questions before God.

WHAT THE MORAL INJURY LENS REVEALS

Reading Habakkuk through the lens of moral injury highlights something easily overlooked. The prophet is not merely uncertain about the future; he is confronting the apparent collapse of justice within the world he inhabits.

God's response eventually reveals that the unfolding of divine justice is more complex than Habakkuk expected. The arrogant powers of the world will not endure forever. Though evil may appear victorious in the present, its downfall is already assured.

Justice is not absent. It is unfolding on a timeline larger than the prophet can see.

This is the context in which the famous declaration appears: "The righteous shall live by faith."

Within the flow of the passage the meaning becomes clearer. Faith means continuing to live faithfully even when the world temporarily appears distorted. Faith does not require pretending injustice does not exist—Habakkuk has already acknowledged that violence and corruption are real.

Instead faith means trusting that the God who governs history has not abandoned the world to chaos. Even when justice appears delayed. Even when evil seems to flourish. Even when life becomes morally confusing.

Habakkuk's journey therefore reveals something profound about the nature of faith. Faith is not the absence of confusion. Faith is the decision to remain in conversation with God when the world no longer makes sense.

HOW THE MORAL INJURY LENS CHANGES THE SERMON

Recognizing the rupture in Habakkuk's experience changes the way this passage can be preached. Without this perspective sermons often move quickly toward reassurance. The preacher reminds the congregation that God is still in control and encourages them to trust God even when circumstances appear confusing.

Those truths are important. Yet when the sermon moves too quickly to reassurance, something essential in the passage can be lost.

Habakkuk does not begin with reassurance. He begins with protest. The prophet stands in the presence of injustice and refuses to pretend that everything makes sense. He names the violence he sees, describes the paralysis of justice, and voices his confusion about why God appears silent.

When preachers allow that tension to remain visible, something important happens in the congregation. People begin to recognize their own questions in the text.

Many believers carry deep confusion about the world around them. They watch injustice unfold in society and wonder why it continues. They see destructive leaders flourish while faithful people struggle. They observe systems that reward greed while punishing integrity.

Experiences like these often produce quiet spiritual turmoil. Believers may feel that their faith has been shaken by what they see, yet they hesitate to speak openly about that struggle. They assume such questions might be inappropriate in church, especially when sermons often emphasize certainty and confidence.

Habakkuk offers something different. The prophet demonstrates that faithful people can bring their confusion directly before God. His protest becomes a model for honest prayer in a broken world.

This recognition changes the tone of the sermon. Instead of rushing to explain injustice, the preacher allows the congregation to sit with the tension of the prophet's question: "How long, O Lord?" This question echoes across generations of believers. It appears in the Psalms, rises in the cries of persecuted communities, and surfaces whenever faithful people confront a world that seems to reward evil while punishing righteousness.

When the sermon acknowledges this tension honestly, it gives the congregation permission to speak truthfully about their own experiences. People who feel disoriented by injustice begin to realize they are not alone. The Bible itself has already given voice to their questions.

The moral injury lens therefore reshapes the sermon in several important ways. First, the sermon becomes more honest. Instead of minimizing injustice, the preacher names it directly. Violence, corruption, and oppression are not abstract ideas in Habakkuk's world, and they are not abstract in ours.

Second, the sermon becomes more pastoral. When people hear Habakkuk's protest they recognize a faith that understands their confusion. The prophet does not stand above the struggle offering simple explanations. He stands within the struggle, asking the same questions many believers carry today.

Third, the sermon becomes more theologically profound. Habakkuk's experience reminds us that divine justice does not always unfold on the timeline we expect. The prophet must learn that God's purposes extend beyond what can be seen in the present moment.

Justice may appear delayed, but it is not absent.

When the sermon reaches this point, hope emerges naturally from the struggle rather than bypassing it. Hope does not appear as a quick answer to a difficult question. Instead it grows out of the long conversation between the prophet and God.

Habakkuk begins with confusion, names the injustice he sees, and wrestles with the delay of divine justice. Through that struggle he discovers that faith can endure even when the world appears morally unstable.

For preachers this approach creates a deeper connection between Scripture and the lives of those listening. The congregation hears a message that does not deny the brokenness of the world. Instead it acknowledges that faithful people sometimes struggle to understand why evil seems to prevail.

Yet the sermon also refuses to surrender to despair. Habakkuk's story shows that believers can bring their deepest questions before God and still discover a path forward.

The prophet does not receive a simple explanation for the injustice he sees. Instead he receives a vision of history that extends beyond the present moment, a vision in which God's justice will ultimately prevail. The powers that dominate the world today will not endure forever, and the righteous are called to live by faith while waiting for that justice to unfold.

When preachers proclaim this message honestly, the congregation hears something deeply needed. Faith does not require pretending that the world always makes sense. Faith means trusting that God is still present even when justice appears delayed.

Habakkuk's protest therefore becomes an invitation. It invites believers to bring their confusion before God, invites the church to speak truthfully about injustice, and invites preachers to proclaim a hope that confronts the brokenness of the world without denying it.

In the sermon that follows, we will see how this passage can be proclaimed in a way that honors the prophet's struggle while pointing the congregation toward the deeper hope found in God's ultimate justice. Habakkuk teaches us that faith sometimes begins with a question: "How long, O Lord?" When that question is spoken honestly before God, it can become the beginning of deeper trust.

SERMON - HOW LONG CAN EVIL WIN?

Text: Habakkuk 1–2

There are moments in life when the world stops making moral sense.

Sometimes those moments come quietly. A person reads the news and sees story after story of corruption, violence, and abuse of power. Someone cheats the system and grows wealthy. A public figure manipulates others and seems untouchable. A destructive leader gains influence while decent people struggle quietly in the background. The headlines accumulate until a troubling question begins to rise in the heart.

Why does evil seem to win?

At other times the question becomes painfully personal. A worker is treated unjustly by an employer and discovers that the system meant to protect them does not work as it should. A family member becomes the victim of crime while the person responsible escapes accountability. Someone who has tried to live honestly and faithfully finds themselves watching dishonest people prosper.

These experiences do more than frustrate us. They disturb something deeper. Most people grow up believing that the world possesses a moral structure. We believe that good actions should lead toward good outcomes. We expect justice to prevail eventually. We trust that wrongdoing will ultimately be exposed and corrected.

Those expectations are not naïve. They arise from something deeply embedded in the human understanding of the world. The biblical story reinforces those instincts by teaching that God is just and that God governs creation with righteousness. The prophets speak about justice rolling down like waters and righteousness like a mighty stream. The Psalms proclaim that the Lord defends the oppressed and brings down the wicked.

Because we believe these things about God, we expect the world to reflect them.

But then we look around and see something very different. Violence spreads across societies. Corruption infiltrates institutions. Those who manipulate power often seem to succeed while those who pursue integrity are left behind.

In those moments people ask a question that has echoed across generations of believers.

How long can evil win?

That is precisely the question the prophet Habakkuk brings before God. The book of Habakkuk opens with one of the most startling prayers in the entire Bible. The prophet surveys the society around him and sees violence, injustice, and corruption spreading across the land. What troubles him most is not simply that evil exists. What troubles him is that God appears silent while it spreads.

Habakkuk cries out to God with remarkable honesty. He asks how long he must call for help without receiving an answer. He wonders why God allows him to witness injustice and tolerate wrongdoing. The prophet describes a world where destruction and conflict are everywhere, where the law has become ineffective, and where justice is distorted because the wicked surround the righteous.

These are not polite religious reflections. They are words of protest spoken directly to God. Habakkuk is not speaking about God in a quiet theological discussion. He is speaking to God with urgency and frustration.

At first glance, such language may sound shocking. Many believers have been taught that faith should avoid questioning God in this way. Some assume that true faith always sounds calm, confident, and certain.

Yet the Bible preserves Habakkuk's protest as part of Scripture. The prophet's words are not removed or softened. They remain in the text because they reveal something important about the nature of faith.

Faith does not always begin with answers.

Sometimes faith begins with a question.

Habakkuk's question arises because he believes something deeply about God. The prophet believes that God is just. He believes that God cares about righteousness and opposes evil. Because he believes this, the reality he sees around him feels unbearable. The moral structure of the world appears broken.

If Habakkuk did not believe in the justice of God, he would have no reason to protest. His complaint exists precisely because he trusts that God is morally consistent. The world should make sense if God governs it with justice.

When it does not, the prophet refuses to ignore the contradiction.

Habakkuk therefore brings his moral confusion directly before God. Instead of pretending that everything is fine, he speaks honestly about what he sees.

Violence is spreading.
Justice is failing.
The wicked appear to be winning.

Many believers today recognize that experience. People often carry these questions quietly within their hearts. They observe injustice in society and wonder why it continues. They see destructive leaders rise to power while people of integrity struggle to be heard. They watch systems reward greed while punishing honesty.

Sometimes those experiences create a quiet spiritual crisis. Believers may wonder whether the world truly reflects the justice of God. Yet they hesitate to voice those questions because they fear sounding unfaithful.

Habakkuk shows us that such questions are not outside the life of faith. The prophet does not abandon his trust in God, but he also refuses to pretend that everything makes sense.

And then something remarkable happens.

God answers.

The response God gives, however, is not what Habakkuk expected. The Lord announces that the Babylonian empire will rise as an instrument of judgment. The Babylonians are powerful conquerors known for brutality and violence. Their armies sweep across nations, leaving destruction behind them.

For Habakkuk, this answer creates an even greater dilemma.

How can a just God use a more wicked nation to punish a less wicked one?

The prophet responds with another protest. He acknowledges that God's eyes are too pure to tolerate evil, yet he cannot understand why God would remain silent while ruthless nations devour those more righteous than themselves.

At this point Habakkuk finds himself standing inside a deep moral tension. The events unfolding in history do not appear to match what he believes about the character of God. The moral logic of the world seems broken.

This experience is not unique to Habakkuk. It appears repeatedly throughout Scripture. The psalmists lament the prosperity of the wicked while the righteous suffer. Job wrestles with the suffering of the innocent. The prophets condemn systems that crush the vulnerable.

The Bible does not hide these struggles. Instead, it preserves them as part of the story of faith.

Habakkuk eventually reaches a turning point in his prayer. After voicing his complaint, he declares that he will stand at his watchpost and wait for

God's response. The image comes from the ancient practice of watchmen standing on city walls scanning the horizon for approaching messengers.

Habakkuk adopts the same posture toward God.

He has spoken honestly about his confusion.

Now he waits.

This waiting becomes the place where God reveals a deeper perspective on history. The Lord declares that the arrogant powers dominating the world will not endure forever. Though Babylon appears unstoppable in the present, its downfall is already assured. The violence it inflicts upon others will eventually return upon itself.

Justice, God reveals, is not absent.

But it unfolds on a timeline larger than human expectations.

Within this context God speaks the words that become central to the book of Habakkuk: "The righteous shall live by faith."

These words do not appear as a simple command to trust God blindly. They emerge from the middle of the prophet's struggle with injustice. Habakkuk has already named the violence and corruption he sees. He has already wrestled with the delay of justice.

Faith does not erase those realities.

Instead, faith becomes the decision to continue trusting God even when the moral order of the world appears temporarily distorted.

Habakkuk begins the book with confusion, but he ends it with a remarkable declaration. In the final chapter the prophet imagines a future in which the fields produce no food and the flocks disappear from the stalls. The economy has collapsed. The visible signs of prosperity have vanished.

Yet Habakkuk declares that even then he will rejoice in the Lord and take joy in the God of his salvation.

This is not the voice of someone who has found easy answers.

It is the voice of someone who has discovered a deeper kind of faith.

Habakkuk has learned that the justice of God may unfold more slowly than human beings expect. The world may appear morally chaotic for a time. Evil may seem powerful. Injustice may appear to prevail.

But those appearances do not tell the entire story.

The Bible ultimately reveals that God's justice unfolds through a history that leads toward a surprising destination. When we continue reading Scripture, we eventually arrive at a moment when injustice appears to triumph in its most shocking form.

Jesus of Nazareth, the most righteous life ever lived, stands before a corrupt court. False accusations are accepted as truth. Political leaders choose expediency over justice. An innocent man is condemned to death.

To the disciples watching these events unfold, it must have seemed as though the moral order of the universe had completely collapsed. The one who healed the sick and welcomed the outcast was executed as a criminal.

Evil appeared to win.

Yet the cross reveals something Habakkuk could only glimpse from a distance. God does not remain detached from the injustice of the world. In Jesus Christ, God enters directly into the suffering and corruption of human history.

The crucifixion shows that God is willing to stand inside the moral chaos of the world rather than abandoning it.

And the resurrection reveals that injustice does not have the final word.

When God raises Jesus from the dead, the verdict of history is overturned. The one condemned as a criminal is vindicated as Lord. The cross becomes the turning point where divine justice begins to overturn the violence and corruption of the world.

The resurrection does not erase the presence of evil in the present world. Violence and injustice still exist. The struggles Habakkuk described have not disappeared.

But the resurrection reveals the direction in which history is moving.

God is restoring the moral order of creation.

The powers that appear dominant today will not endure forever. The injustice that wounds the world will not ultimately prevail. The God who raised Jesus from the dead is bringing history toward a future where righteousness and peace will finally prevail.

This is why Christians continue to live by faith even when the world seems morally confusing.

Faith does not mean pretending that injustice is acceptable. Habakkuk teaches us to name injustice honestly and bring our questions before God. Faith also does not mean believing that evil will immediately disappear.

Instead, faith means trusting that the God who governs history is still at work even when the timeline of justice remains hidden from us.

The righteous live by faith because they believe that the story of the world is not finished.

Habakkuk began with a question that echoes across the centuries.

How long can evil win?

The answer Scripture gives is both sobering and hopeful.

Evil may appear powerful for a time.

Injustice may seem to flourish.

But the God who governs history has not surrendered the world to chaos.

Justice will come.

And until that day arrives, the people of God continue to live by faith, trusting that the God who hears the cries of prophets and raises the dead is still writing the final chapter of the story.

Chapter 4

When the Good Suffer

Text: Job 1–2; 38–42

OPENING PASTORAL SCENARIO: WHEN THE GOOD SUFFER

Every pastor eventually sits with someone who asks a question that has no easy answer.

The setting may be a hospital room where a family waits anxiously for news, a quiet conversation after a funeral, or a moment in a church office when someone finally voices what they have been carrying for weeks. The question usually comes slowly, almost cautiously.

"I don't understand. They are such a good person. Why would this happen to them?"

Pastors hear this question often because it touches something deep within the human heart. People naturally expect the world to operate with moral coherence. We assume kindness should matter, integrity should count for something, and faithfulness should not lead toward suffering. When someone who has lived destructively encounters painful consequences, the situation may be tragic but it still feels understandable. The outcome appears connected to the choices that were made. But when someone who is genuinely good suffers deeply, the experience feels different. Something about it seems wrong, as though the moral order of the world has fractured.

Most believers carry some version of this expectation about life. It is rarely stated explicitly, yet it shapes how many people understand the relationship between faith and experience. Deep down we often assume that living faithfully should lead toward stability, protection, or blessing.

That assumption has strong roots in the biblical story itself. Scripture frequently connects obedience with life and disobedience with destruction. The wisdom literature often describes righteousness leading toward flourishing while wickedness leads toward ruin. Because of these themes, many believers quietly expect goodness and blessing to appear together.

Yet life does not always follow that pattern.

Sometimes the most faithful people encounter the deepest suffering. Those who serve others selflessly may still experience loss, illness, or hardship. People who love God sincerely sometimes find themselves walking through seasons that feel overwhelmingly difficult.

When those experiences occur, the result is not only grief but confusion. People begin to question the moral order of the world. If God is just, why do the righteous suffer? If faithfulness matters, why does it sometimes seem to make no difference?

The Bible does not avoid these questions.

In fact, one of the longest books in Scripture is devoted entirely to exploring them.

The book of Job confronts one of the most painful dilemmas believers face: the suffering of the innocent. It tells the story of a man described as blameless and upright, someone who fears God and turns away from evil. Job is not portrayed as morally ambiguous or spiritually careless. From the opening chapter, the narrative presents him as a person of deep integrity.

Yet Job's life is suddenly overwhelmed by devastating loss. The narrative moves quickly, and the stability that once defined his world disappears. By the end of the opening chapters, the man who once lived in prosperity now sits in ashes, struggling to understand what has happened.

From Job's perspective, nothing about the situation makes moral sense.

He has not abandoned God or turned toward wrongdoing. His life has been marked by faithfulness, yet suffering has entered his story in a way that seems completely disconnected from his character. The problem is not simply that Job is suffering. The deeper issue is that his suffering appears undeserved.

If goodness does not protect a person from suffering, how are we supposed to understand the relationship between righteousness and life?

This is the question the book of Job forces us to confront.

For centuries believers have wrestled with this story because it speaks directly to one of the deepest wounds of human experience. When people see the righteous suffer, something inside them struggles to reconcile that reality with their belief in a just God. The result can be profound spiritual tension.

Many people attempt to resolve that tension by searching for explanations. Friends and family members may suggest hidden reasons for the suffering. Some assume the person must have done something wrong. Others suggest the suffering must serve some greater purpose that will eventually become clear.

These responses are understandable. Human beings naturally want the world to make sense.

But the book of Job challenges that instinct.

The story unfolds in a way that refuses easy explanations. As Job's friends attempt to interpret his suffering, their arguments repeatedly fail to capture the truth of the situation. They insist suffering must result from wrongdoing, yet the narrative itself has already told us that Job is innocent.

The tension remains unresolved.

Job therefore becomes one of the clearest examples of moral rupture in Scripture. The world Job believed he understood no longer operates according to the expectations he trusted.

This is precisely the kind of moment where the concept of moral injury helps us read the text more clearly.

Moral injury occurs when deeply held moral expectations are violated by reality. Something happens that contradicts the way the world should work. The result is not simply emotional pain but a deeper crisis involving meaning, justice, and trust.

Job experiences exactly this kind of rupture.

The man who believed righteousness mattered now finds himself suffering in ways that appear disconnected from his character. His friends attempt to restore the moral order of the world by insisting that Job must have done something wrong.

But Job knows that explanation is not true.

And so the story moves into a long conversation about justice, suffering, and faith.

Before we explore that conversation, we must recognize the remarkable honesty of the biblical text. The book of Job does not avoid the painful question of undeserved suffering. Instead it places that question at the very center of the narrative.

In doing so, Scripture acknowledges something pastors encounter regularly.

Sometimes good people suffer.

Sometimes faithfulness does not prevent hardship.

Sometimes the moral order of the world appears deeply confusing.

The story of Job invites us to wrestle with those realities rather than dismiss them. It reminds us that faith does not always provide simple explanations for suffering. Instead, faith sometimes begins by acknowledging that the world we experience does not always match the expectations we carry.

This is where Job's journey begins.

The man who once lived within a world that seemed morally coherent now finds himself in a place where nothing makes sense. His experience forces him to confront a question believers across generations have asked.

What does faith look like when the good suffer?

THE PASSAGE AS WE USUALLY PREACH IT

When pastors preach the book of Job, the message often centers on trusting God in difficult circumstances. Job is presented as a model of perseverance, a man who continues to worship even when everything in his life collapses.

Many sermons highlight Job's famous response after the first wave of tragedy:

"The Lord gave, and the Lord has taken away; blessed be the name of the Lord" (Job 1:21).

These words reveal remarkable faith, and for that reason Job is frequently presented as an example of steadfast devotion. The sermon often follows a familiar pattern: when suffering enters our lives, we should respond as Job did and continue trusting God.

There is truth in that message. The opening chapters of Job portray a man who refuses to curse God even in devastating grief.

Yet if the sermon stops there, it misses most of the book.

The story of Job does not end with quiet endurance. The opening chapters only introduce the crisis that unfolds across the rest of the narrative. After the initial silence of mourning, Job begins to speak, and his words reveal a struggle far more complex than simple patience.

Job does not quietly accept his suffering. He laments the day he was born, questions the meaning of his pain, and searches desperately for some explanation that might make sense of his life. The book therefore presents a far more complex portrait of faith than the one often described in sermons.

Job struggles.

He questions.

He protests.

These responses reveal the deep moral turmoil created by his suffering.

Much of the book is devoted to conversations between Job and his friends. They arrive intending to comfort him, sitting silently beside him for seven days. But once they begin speaking, the discussion shifts toward explanation.

The friends believe suffering must be connected to wrongdoing. Their reasoning reflects a moral framework common in ancient wisdom traditions: righteousness leads toward blessing while wrongdoing leads toward suffering.

According to this logic, Job's situation can only have one explanation.

He must have done something wrong.

The friends never accuse him of a specific sin, but they repeatedly imply that hidden failure must exist somewhere in his life. Their speeches defend a predictable moral system in which suffering corresponds directly to wrongdoing.

At first their reasoning sounds persuasive. Scripture often affirms that God cares about righteousness and that destructive choices carry consequences.

But the reader already knows something the friends do not.

The narrative has already declared that Job is innocent.

Their explanation therefore cannot account for what has happened.

And so the tension of the story deepens.

Job insists that their explanation does not match reality. The friends insist that their moral framework must still be correct. Their debate becomes the central conflict of the book.

The issue is not simply that Job is suffering.

The deeper issue is that his suffering appears undeserved.

When the moral logic people rely on to interpret the world fails, confusion inevitably follows. The book of Job forces readers to confront that moment directly.

A good man suffers.

And the usual explanations do not work.

THE MORAL INJURY QUESTION: WHERE DOES THE MORAL WORLD BREAK?

At this point in the chapter we ask the interpretive question that has guided our reading throughout this book:

Where does the moral world appear to break in this passage?

In the story of Job, the rupture is unmistakable.

A righteous man suffers.

That simple reality contains the entire crisis of the book. Job is introduced as "blameless and upright, one who fears God and turns away from evil" (Job 1:1). The narrator carefully establishes his character before the story unfolds so that readers will understand from the beginning that Job is a person of deep integrity.

Yet almost immediately his life collapses. Stability disappears, and the world that once seemed morally coherent becomes unrecognizable.

The suffering itself is not the deepest issue.

The deeper issue is that Job cannot connect his suffering to any wrongdoing.

For much of human history people have relied on a fairly simple moral framework for interpreting life. Good actions lead toward good outcomes, while harmful actions eventually produce painful consequences. Wisdom traditions across cultures reflect this expectation. Proverbs, for example, frequently describes a world in which righteousness leads toward life while wickedness leads toward ruin.

This framework provides a sense of moral coherence. If the world operates this way, life appears understandable and events can be interpreted according to predictable patterns.

But Job's experience does not fit that pattern.

He has lived faithfully, yet he suffers deeply.

When Job's friends arrive, they immediately attempt to restore the moral logic that appears to have collapsed. Their speeches reflect the same framework we have just described. They insist that God governs the world with justice and that suffering must therefore be connected to wrongdoing.

Their reasoning is straightforward.

If Job is suffering, he must have sinned.

Perhaps some hidden wrongdoing exists. Perhaps he has overlooked a moral failure. The friends urge him to examine his life and repent so that restoration can occur.

At first glance their reasoning may sound persuasive. Scripture frequently teaches that God cares deeply about righteousness and that wrongdoing carries consequences.

But the reader already knows something Job's friends do not.

The opening chapters of the book have already declared that Job is innocent.

The narrative itself therefore exposes the weakness of the friends' reasoning. Their moral framework cannot explain what is happening. The system they rely upon no longer holds.

This is where the concept of moral injury becomes especially helpful.

Moral injury occurs when deeply held expectations about the moral order of the world collapse. Something happens that contradicts the way reality should work. The result is not simply emotional pain but a crisis of meaning.

Job experiences exactly this kind of rupture.

He believed righteousness mattered. He believed the world reflected the justice of God. Those convictions shaped the way he understood his life.

Now that framework appears shattered.

Job cannot reconcile his suffering with the moral order he trusted. If righteousness does not lead toward flourishing, what does righteousness mean? If suffering is not connected to wrongdoing, how should the events of life be interpreted?

These questions are not abstract philosophical puzzles.

They are deeply personal.

Job's suffering forces him to confront the possibility that the world may not operate according to the moral expectations he once trusted.

This explains the intensity of his conversations with his friends. They are trying to preserve a stable explanation for suffering. If they can convince Job that he has sinned, then the moral order still makes sense.

Righteousness leads to blessing.

Wrongdoing leads to suffering.

But Job refuses that explanation.

He knows his own life, and he knows the accusations implied by his friends do not match reality. Instead of accepting their reasoning, he insists on speaking honestly about what he is experiencing.

This honesty becomes one of the most striking features of the book.

Job laments his suffering openly. He questions the fairness of what has happened and at times challenges God to explain the situation. These words may sound uncomfortable to modern readers, but they reveal the depth of his struggle.

Job is not merely grieving his losses.

He is trying to understand how the moral order of the world can still make sense.

Many believers today encounter similar moments of confusion. When good people suffer deeply, observers often search for explanations that restore moral coherence. We hear statements such as "There must be a reason for this" or "Everything happens for a purpose." These responses usually arise from compassion, but they also reveal a desire to preserve the idea that the world ultimately makes sense.

If suffering can be explained, the moral order remains intact.

But the book of Job challenges this instinct.

The story repeatedly demonstrates that easy explanations do not resolve the tension of suffering. Job's friends continue offering theological arguments, yet none of them truly address the depth of the crisis.

The rupture remains.

Job therefore becomes one of the most powerful voices of protest in Scripture. He refuses explanations that deny the reality of his experience and continues speaking honestly about his confusion.

At one point Job declares that he wishes he could present his case before God directly. He longs for a conversation in which the apparent injustice of his situation could finally be addressed.

This desire reveals something profound about Job's faith.

Despite his confusion, he has not abandoned God.

He still believes that God is just. That conviction is precisely why the situation troubles him so deeply. If God were indifferent to justice, the suffering might simply be meaningless.

But Job believes God is righteous.

And so he demands an answer.

This tension between faith and confusion lies at the heart of the book. Job refuses to abandon his belief in God's justice, yet he also refuses to ignore the reality that the world appears unjust.

The result is a long and emotionally intense search for understanding.

Sometimes the good suffer.

Sometimes life unfolds in ways that contradict the moral expectations we carry.

In those moments believers may experience a deep spiritual rupture. The world that once seemed morally coherent suddenly becomes confusing.

The book of Job does not rush to repair that rupture.

Instead it allows the tension to remain visible.

And in doing so it prepares us for one of the most remarkable encounters in Scripture.

After many chapters of debate and lament, God finally speaks.

But the answer God gives is not what anyone expects.

WHAT THE MORAL INJURY LENS REVEALS

Reading the book of Job through the lens of moral injury brings a crucial insight into focus.

The deepest struggle in the book is not simply the presence of suffering. Human beings have always experienced hardship, loss, and grief. Scripture never denies that these realities exist in a broken world.

The deeper struggle in Job is the collapse of a moral framework that once seemed reliable.

Job believed righteousness mattered and that the world reflected the justice of God. Within that framework suffering could usually be explained. Hardship might be connected to wrongdoing, discipline, or the consequences of destructive choices.

But Job's experience does not fit any of those explanations.

A good man suffers.

That simple fact creates the central crisis of the book.

The speeches of Job's friends represent the human instinct to repair a broken moral framework. They insist that suffering must always have a moral explanation because their theology depends on preserving a predictable relationship between righteousness and blessing.

If someone experiences great suffering, there must be a corresponding moral failure somewhere in the story.

Yet the narrative repeatedly shows that this explanation cannot account for Job's experience.

The friends are trying to protect their understanding of how the world works. If Job's suffering is undeserved, then the entire system they trust begins to unravel.

This explains the intensity of their arguments.

Job's experience threatens their moral certainty.

The book of Job therefore exposes a tension that appears throughout Scripture. Many passages affirm that righteousness leads toward life and wrongdoing eventually leads toward destruction. These themes remain true and important within the biblical story.

But Job reminds us that these patterns do not function as simple formulas.

Sometimes the righteous suffer.

Sometimes the wicked flourish for a time.

When those realities appear, believers may experience the kind of rupture we describe as moral injury.

This insight becomes especially clear in Job's response to his suffering. He refuses explanations that deny the reality of what has happened. His friends attempt to restore moral order by insisting that hidden sin must be present, but Job knows that explanation is false.

Instead of surrendering to their reasoning, Job insists on telling the truth about his experience. He laments, questions, and continues demanding that his suffering be taken seriously.

These responses may feel uncomfortable, but they reveal something profound about faith.

Job's protest is not the rejection of God.

It is the refusal to accept explanations that misrepresent reality.

Job believes God is just. That conviction is precisely why he cannot accept the arguments of his friends. If God is truly just, the explanations they offer cannot be correct.

Job's protest therefore arises from his commitment to the moral character of God.

This insight becomes clearer when God finally speaks. The Lord does not provide a detailed explanation for Job's suffering. Instead God describes the vast complexity of creation—the foundations of the earth, the boundaries of the sea, the movements of the stars, and the lives of creatures beyond human control.

At first this response appears unrelated to Job's questions, but the message becomes clearer as the speech unfolds.

God is revealing that the moral and physical order of creation is far larger than Job imagined. The universe cannot be reduced to simple formulas that human beings can easily understand. Divine justice operates within a reality whose complexity extends far beyond human perspective.

This does not mean that God's justice is absent.

It means that God's justice unfolds within a world far more intricate than human reasoning can fully grasp.

The friends attempted to force suffering into a simplified moral system.

God reveals that creation is far larger than such explanations allow.

By the end of the book God rebukes the friends and declares that they have not spoken rightly about Him as Job has. Their confident explanations misrepresented the complexity of reality.

Job, however, remained honest. He refused false answers and continued seeking God even when the moral order of the world appeared broken.

The result is a deeper form of faith.

Job no longer relies on a predictable moral system. Instead he trusts the character of the God he has encountered.

His faith has moved from certainty about how the world works to trust in the wisdom of God.

HOW THE MORAL INJURY LENS CHANGES THE SERMON

Recognizing the moral rupture in Job's story changes the way this passage can be preached.

Many sermons approach the book primarily as a lesson about patience and endurance. Job becomes an example of perseverance, and the congregation is encouraged to follow his example by trusting God during difficult circumstances.

While that message contains truth, it can overlook the deeper struggle that occupies most of the narrative.

The book of Job is not simply a story about patience followed by blessing.

It is a sustained exploration of moral confusion.

Most of the book is devoted to the painful dialogue between Job and his friends as they wrestle with the problem of undeserved suffering.

When preachers recognize this, the tone of the sermon begins to change.

Instead of presenting Job as a simple model of endurance, the preacher acknowledges the rupture at the center of the story. A righteous man suffers in ways that appear disconnected from his character, and the moral expectations people often rely upon to interpret the world collapse.

This recognition immediately makes the passage more relatable.

In nearly every congregation there are individuals who have experienced suffering that does not seem to make moral sense. They tried to live faithfully, yet their lives were still touched by loss, illness, disappointment, or hardship.

When sermons rush to explain suffering too quickly, they can unintentionally repeat the mistake of Job's friends.

The moral injury lens encourages a different approach.

Instead of offering immediate explanations, the sermon acknowledges the tension preserved in the text itself. Sometimes the suffering of the righteous cannot be easily explained. The world does not always operate according to the simple formulas we would prefer.

When the sermon names this tension honestly, something important happens within the congregation.

People feel seen.

Those who have struggled with undeserved suffering recognize that Scripture understands their experience. The Bible does not pretend that the world always makes sense. Instead it preserves the voices of those who wrestled deeply with that confusion.

Job's story therefore gives believers permission to speak honestly about their pain.

The sermon becomes a place where lament is allowed.

Faith does not require pretending that suffering always makes sense.

Faith sometimes means continuing to seek God even when the moral order of the world appears confusing.

For many listeners this recognition brings relief. Their questions no longer feel like evidence of weak faith. Instead they recognize that their struggle places them within the long story of believers who wrestled with the same tensions.

And in that struggle they may discover what Job ultimately discovered:

Even when the world feels morally confusing,

God is still present.

The world may sometimes appear morally disordered.

But the God who governs creation has not abandoned the story.

Job's journey therefore invites us to bring our deepest questions before God. Instead of pretending that life always makes sense, we can speak honestly about our confusion and grief. Scripture assures us that such honesty does not weaken faith; it often becomes the place where faith grows deeper.

When the good suffer, the answer is not found in simple explanations.

It is found in the presence of the God who hears the cry of His people and whose wisdom ultimately holds the world together.

And in that presence, faith continues to live—even in a world that does not always make sense.

SERMON - WHEN THE GOOD SUFFER

Scripture: Job 1–2; 38–42

There are moments in life when suffering raises a question that seems almost impossible to answer. It is the question people whisper in hospital rooms, ask quietly after funerals, and sometimes carry silently for years. The question often begins simply enough, but behind it lies a deeper struggle about how the world works.

Why do good people suffer?

Most of us assume, even if we have never said it out loud, that the world should operate with some kind of moral order. We believe that kindness should matter, that integrity should count for something, and that faithfulness should not lead toward devastation. When people who act selfishly or destructively experience painful consequences, the situation may still be tragic, but it usually feels understandable. The outcome seems connected to the choices that were made. When someone who has lived faithfully suffers deeply, however, the experience feels very different. Something about it seems wrong, as though the moral fabric of the world has been torn.

The book of Job confronts that experience directly. It tells the story of a man who appears to embody everything that wisdom literature celebrates. Job is introduced as blameless and upright, a man who fears God and turns away from evil. He is responsible in his work, attentive to his family, and deeply concerned about honoring God in every part of his life. The opening chapters present him as the kind of person who seems to live within the blessing of a just and ordered world.

Yet almost immediately the story takes a devastating turn. In a series of rapid reports, everything that once defined Job's life disappears. Raiders steal his livestock. Fire destroys his flocks. A violent storm collapses the house where his children are gathered, and all of them die. In the span of a few moments the world that once appeared stable becomes unrecognizable. The man who once stood at the center of a thriving household now stands alone in grief.

The story continues to deepen the crisis. Soon Job himself becomes afflicted with painful sores that cover his body from head to foot. He sits in ashes outside the city, scraping his skin with broken pottery. The image is stark and unsettling. A man who once lived within prosperity and dignity now sits surrounded by loss and pain.

What makes Job's suffering so difficult is not simply its intensity. The deeper issue is that it appears undeserved. The narrative has already made it clear that Job is not being punished for wrongdoing. The reader knows something the characters in the story do not: Job's suffering is not the result of moral failure. A good man suffers, and the usual explanations do not work.

At first Job responds with remarkable restraint. After the first wave of tragedy, he tears his robe, shaves his head, and falls to the ground in grief. Yet in the midst of that sorrow he declares, "The Lord gave, and the Lord has taken away; blessed be the name of the Lord." Those words have echoed through centuries because they reveal extraordinary faith in the face of unimaginable loss.

But the story does not end there. As the days pass, Job begins to speak again, and his words reveal a man wrestling deeply with what has happened to him. He curses the day of his birth. He questions the meaning of his suffering. He searches for some explanation that might help him understand why his life has taken such a devastating turn.

When Job's friends arrive, the crisis enters a new phase. At first their presence seems compassionate. They sit with him in silence for seven days, sharing his grief. Sometimes the most faithful thing we can do for someone who is suffering is simply to sit beside them without trying to fix what cannot yet be explained.

Eventually, however, the friends begin to speak, and their words reveal how deeply the question of suffering troubles them as well. They believe that the world operates according to a clear moral order. God governs the world with justice, they insist, and therefore suffering must be connected to wrongdoing. If Job is experiencing such overwhelming loss, then some hidden sin must exist in his life.

Their reasoning follows a pattern that many people still recognize. If the world is morally ordered, then suffering must have a cause that fits within that order. The friends encourage Job to examine his life carefully, to search for whatever wrongdoing may have brought this disaster upon him. If he repents, they suggest, restoration will surely follow.

At first their arguments sound convincing because much of what they say echoes themes found elsewhere in Scripture. The Bible often affirms that righteousness leads toward life and that destructive choices eventually bring painful consequences. Yet in Job's case those explanations do not fit.

Job knows it, and the reader knows it as well.

The man sitting in ashes has not turned away from God. His suffering cannot be explained by the logic his friends defend. The moral system they rely upon has failed to account for what has happened.

As the conversation continues, the tension grows. Job refuses to accept their explanation, and the friends refuse to abandon their understanding of how the world works. The debate becomes increasingly intense. Job laments his suffering openly. He questions the fairness of what has happened. At times he even cries out to God, longing for the chance to present his case directly before the Creator.

Some readers feel uneasy about the boldness of Job's words. Yet the Bible preserves his protest as part of the story of faith. Scripture does not silence his struggle or smooth it over with quick explanations. Instead, it allows Job's voice to remain in the conversation.

This honesty is one of the most remarkable features of the book.

Eventually, after many chapters of argument and lament, something extraordinary happens. God speaks.

Throughout the story Job has longed for an answer. He has imagined standing before God and presenting his case. Now the Lord answers him from a whirlwind. The moment is dramatic and mysterious. The God who seemed silent through so much of the story suddenly addresses the suffering man directly.

But the response God gives is not what Job—or the reader—might expect.

God does not offer a detailed explanation for Job's suffering. He does not reveal the heavenly conversation that took place before the tragedies began. Instead, the Lord begins describing the vastness and complexity of creation.

Where were you when the foundations of the earth were laid?

Can you command the morning to appear?

Do you know the paths of the stars or the depths of the sea?

The speech moves across the world of creation: mountains and oceans, storms and constellations, wild animals and distant horizons. The images are sweeping and powerful. God is revealing a universe that is far larger and more intricate than Job had ever imagined.

At first this response may seem puzzling. Job asked why he was suffering, and God responds by describing the structure of the cosmos. Yet as the speech continues, a deeper message begins to emerge.

God is revealing that the world cannot be reduced to the simple formulas Job's friends tried to defend. Creation is vast and complex. The moral life of the world unfolds within a reality far larger than human understanding can fully grasp.

This does not mean that justice does not exist. It does not mean that God is indifferent to suffering or unconcerned with righteousness. Instead, it means that the justice of God operates within a story whose scope extends far beyond what human beings can easily see.

Job's friends assumed that suffering must always correspond directly to wrongdoing. Their explanation depended on a predictable moral system. God's response reveals that the world is far more complex than that system allowed.

Sometimes the righteous suffer.

Sometimes the wicked flourish for a time.

The justice of God is real, but it unfolds within a creation whose complexity surpasses human understanding.

At the end of the story, something surprising happens. God rebukes Job's friends. The Lord declares that they have not spoken rightly about Him, even though they tried so hard to defend divine justice. Their explanations were too confident, too certain that they understood how the world worked.

Job, however, is not condemned for his protest. Despite all his questions and lament, he remained honest about what he was experiencing. He refused to accept explanations that distorted the truth of his life. He continued seeking God even when the moral order of the world seemed broken.

In the end Job responds with humility. He acknowledges that the wisdom of God extends beyond his understanding. Yet something important has changed. Earlier in the story, Job believed he understood how the world worked. By the end of the book, his faith rests not in a predictable system but in the character of God Himself.

This shift lies at the heart of the book of Job.

Job's faith moves from confidence in a moral formula to trust in the living God.

That movement speaks directly to believers today.

Many people begin the life of faith believing that obedience and blessing will always move together in predictable ways. We hope that living faithfully will protect us from the worst forms of suffering. Yet life sometimes confronts us with experiences that do not fit that expectation.

When those moments arrive, faith can feel fragile. We begin to wonder whether the story we believed about God and the world still makes sense.

The book of Job suggests that faith does not require having every answer to the mystery of suffering. Instead, faith sometimes grows through the struggle to trust God even when life becomes difficult to understand.

Job never receives a full explanation for what happened to him. The mystery remains. Yet he encounters God in a way that changes how he understands the world. The presence of God becomes more significant than the answers he once sought.

For many believers, that truth becomes deeply comforting.

People who have walked through suffering often discover that simple explanations rarely satisfy the deepest questions of the heart. What they long for most is not a formula that explains everything, but the assurance that God has not abandoned them.

The story of Job offers that assurance.

The God who speaks from the whirlwind is not distant from human suffering. The Lord who created the stars and seas is the same God who listens to the cries of those who suffer.

And the larger story of Scripture reveals something even more astonishing.

The deepest example of undeserved suffering does not appear in the book of Job. It appears in the life of Jesus Christ.

At the cross, the most righteous life ever lived was condemned by an unjust world. The one who embodied perfect faithfulness to God suffered violence, rejection, and death.

If suffering always reflected wrongdoing, the cross would make no sense.

Yet the resurrection reveals that God's justice operates within a story far greater than human understanding.

The God who spoke to Job from the whirlwind is the same God who raises the dead.

And because of that truth, believers can continue to trust even when life becomes morally confusing.

The mystery of suffering remains, but the presence of God remains as well. And it is within that presence that faith continues to live.

PART II

LEARNING TO SPEAK IN THE RUPTURE

Chapter 5

How Long, O Lord?

Text: Psalm 13

OPENING PASTORAL SCENARIO: WHEN THE SILENCE FEELS LONG

There are seasons in the life of faith when the hardest part is not suffering itself but the silence that surrounds it.

A person prays for clarity about a difficult decision and hears nothing. Someone cries out for help in the middle of a painful season, yet the situation does not change. A family waits for relief from a long struggle, but the days continue to unfold without any visible answer. Over time the question begins to rise quietly within the heart:

How long, O Lord?

Pastors hear that question in many forms. It may come from someone who has been waiting for healing for years. It may come from a believer praying for reconciliation in a broken relationship. At other times it comes from someone who has watched injustice continue while the prayers of the faithful seem to rise into an empty sky.

Experiences like these can be deeply unsettling because many believers expect prayer to lead to visible responses from God. When those responses do not appear, the silence itself becomes a source of spiritual tension. People begin to wonder whether their prayers matter, whether God truly hears them, or whether something has gone wrong in their faith.

Yet the Bible contains many voices that speak from precisely this place.

One of the clearest examples appears in Psalm 13, a short but powerful prayer that captures the experience of waiting for God in the midst of distress. The psalm opens with a cry that has echoed through centuries of worship:

"How long, O Lord?
Will you forget me forever?
How long will you hide your face from me?" (Ps 13:1).

These words can sound shocking at first. The psalmist addresses God with remarkable honesty, expressing a sense of abandonment that many believers hesitate to voice. Yet Scripture preserves this prayer without apology. The Bible includes this cry as part of the language of faith.

Psalm 13 belongs to the larger family of lament psalms. These prayers arise when the world no longer feels morally coherent. The writer experiences suffering, opposition, or injustice and brings that pain directly into the presence of God. What makes these prayers so striking is their honesty. They do not pretend that everything is fine, nor do they suppress the emotional weight of the situation. Instead, they place the full reality of human struggle before the Lord.

This is an important step in the biblical story we have been tracing.

Earlier chapters have explored moments when the moral structure of the world appears to fracture. Abraham faced the unthinkable command that tested his faith. Habakkuk wrestled with injustice spreading through society. Job confronted the suffering of the innocent and struggled to reconcile that suffering with his belief in divine justice.

Now Scripture introduces another dimension of moral rupture: the experience of divine silence.

The psalmist of Psalm 13 is not merely enduring hardship. The deeper struggle is the absence of divine response. Prayers have been spoken, yet the situation remains unchanged, creating the painful impression that God has turned away.

"How long will you hide your face from me?"

In the language of the Old Testament, the "face" of God represents divine presence and favor. When God's face shines upon someone, it signifies blessing and protection. When God hides His face, the experience feels like abandonment. The psalmist therefore describes a deeply personal spiritual distress: the unsettling sense of being forgotten.

The struggle soon moves inward as well.

"How long must I wrestle with my thoughts
and day after day have sorrow in my heart?" (verse 2a).

Here the psalmist describes the internal turmoil created by unanswered prayer. The absence of divine response produces a relentless cycle of questions. The mind returns again and again to the same uncertainty, searching for answers that never quite appear.

Many believers recognize this experience. When prayers seem unanswered, people begin examining themselves. They ask whether they prayed correctly, whether their faith is strong enough, or whether something in their lives has created distance between themselves and God. Such questions easily spiral into discouragement.

The psalmist then introduces another dimension of distress:

"How long will my enemy triumph over me?" (verse 2b).

Now personal suffering intersects with external opposition. The psalmist faces pressure from others, and the apparent success of those opponents intensifies the sense that God has not intervened.

The situation feels morally disordered. The faithful suffer while the opposition appears strong, and God seems silent.

This is precisely where the moral injury lens becomes helpful. The deepest wound in Psalm 13 is not merely the presence of hardship but the tension between what the psalmist believes about God and what he experiences in the present moment.

The writer believes that God hears prayer, cares about justice, and defends the faithful. When those convictions collide with the experience of unanswered prayer, the result is spiritual disorientation. The moral structure of the world suddenly feels uncertain.

Psalm 13 gives voice to that experience.

Rather than hiding the struggle, the psalm places it at the center of prayer. The writer speaks honestly about the sense of abandonment, the turmoil within his own thoughts, and the apparent triumph of opposition.

This honesty is one of the most remarkable features of the biblical tradition. Many religious systems encourage people to hide doubt or maintain a polished image of faith. Scripture often does the opposite, preserving prayers that speak openly about confusion, frustration, and longing.

Psalm 13 therefore invites believers into a form of prayer marked by honesty. The psalmist does not abandon faith, but neither does he pretend that everything makes sense. Instead, he brings his confusion directly to God.

"How long, O Lord?"

That question echoes across generations. It arises in moments of personal suffering, in communities facing injustice, and in the hearts of believers who have waited longer than they expected for God's help.

Psalm 13 reminds us that such questions belong within the life of faith.

The psalmist does not speak these words about God to others. He speaks them directly to God. This distinction matters. The lament is not disbelief but relationship. Only someone who still believes God hears prayer would cry out with such urgency.

The protest therefore reveals a faith that refuses to abandon the conversation with God.

In the next section we will consider how this passage is usually preached and why familiar interpretations sometimes move too quickly past the raw honesty of the psalm.

THE PASSAGE AS WE USUALLY PREACH IT

When Psalm 13 appears in sermons, the message often moves quickly toward its conclusion.

This is understandable because the final verses sound hopeful and reassuring:

"But I trust in your unfailing love;
my heart rejoices in your salvation.
I will sing the Lord's praise,
for he has been good to me." (verses 5–6).

Because the psalm ends with confidence, sermons frequently emphasize the movement from despair to trust. The message becomes simple and encouraging: even when life feels difficult, believers should remember God's goodness and choose to trust Him.

That interpretation contains genuine truth. Psalm 13 does end with an affirmation of trust, and the writer does turn toward hope. Yet when sermons focus primarily on the ending, they can unintentionally minimize the depth of the struggle that fills the opening lines.

The questions that dominate the beginning of the psalm are not brief emotional outbursts. They are the heart of the prayer.

Four times the same question appears:

How long?

How long, O Lord?

How long will you forget me?

How long will you hide your face from me?

How long must I wrestle with my thoughts?

How long will my enemy triumph over me?

The repetition is deliberate. The psalmist asks the question again and again, allowing the weight of waiting to fill the prayer.

Yet sermons often soften that repetition. The preacher may acknowledge the question briefly before assuring the congregation that God's timing can be trusted. In doing so, the lament becomes a passing emotional moment rather than a profound theological struggle.

This pattern reflects a broader tendency in modern preaching. Many pastors feel uncomfortable lingering within unresolved questions. Congregations often expect sermons to provide clarity and encouragement, so preachers naturally move toward reassurance.

Psalm 13, however, invites us to remain for a moment within the tension of waiting.

The psalmist does not begin with confidence but with confusion. He feels forgotten, experiences sorrow day after day, sees his enemies gaining strength, and senses that God has hidden His face.

This is not a mild emotional disturbance but a spiritual crisis.

The psalmist's understanding of God's relationship with His people has been shaken. The covenant tradition taught that God hears the cries of the faithful and acts on their behalf, yet the present experience appears to contradict that expectation.

The result is moral disorientation.

God seems distant. Justice appears delayed. The waiting feels endless.

If we move too quickly to the psalm's closing words of trust, we risk missing the significance of this tension. The transformation at the end of the prayer becomes meaningful only when we first recognize how deep the struggle truly is.

Another common preaching approach interprets the lament primarily as an expression of emotion. In this view the psalmist becomes a model for emotional honesty in prayer, demonstrating that believers can bring sadness and discouragement to God.

This interpretation captures an important insight. The psalms certainly encourage honest expression before God. Yet the distress described in Psalm 13 is not merely emotional; it is moral and theological.

The psalmist believes God is just and attentive. When that conviction collides with divine silence, the result is confusion about how the world works.

Why does God appear absent?

Why does injustice continue?

Why must the faithful carry sorrow day after day?

These questions challenge the believer's understanding of God's involvement in the world. When sermons treat Psalm 13 primarily as a lesson in emotional expression, they may unintentionally bypass the deeper tension preserved within the text.

The psalm is not only about sadness.

It is about the collapse of a moral expectation.

The writer expected God to act. He believed justice would prevail and assumed that the faithful would not remain forgotten.

When those expectations remain unmet, the result is a spiritual wound. The question "How long?" expresses that wound. It is the cry of someone who still believes in God's justice but cannot yet see it operating in the present moment.

This insight prepares us for the central diagnostic question of this chapter:

Where does the moral world appear to break in this passage?

Absolutely. Below is the completed pass for the remaining three sections of Chapter 5, with the same treatment applied throughout:

- clarity pass
- repetition pass
- global phrase pass
- compression / density pass
- final polish

I preserved your argument, tone, and overall length while reducing white space, smoothing transitions, and tightening repeated phrasing.

THE MORAL INJURY QUESTION: WHERE DOES THE MORAL WORLD BREAK?

At this point in each chapter we ask the diagnostic question that helps us read the text through the lens of moral injury:

Where does the moral world appear to break in this passage?

This question slows us down. Instead of moving quickly toward resolution, it asks us to pay attention to the moment when expectations about God and the world begin to fracture.

When we apply that question to Psalm 13, the answer becomes clear almost immediately.

The rupture appears in the psalmist's repeated cry:

"How long, O Lord?"

The question itself reveals that something has gone wrong.

In the moral world the psalmist expects, God does not forget His people. He does not hide His face indefinitely. He hears the cries of the faithful and acts on their behalf.

That expectation runs throughout the story of Scripture. In the Exodus narrative, God hears the suffering of Israel and delivers them from oppression. In the covenant promises, God assures His people that He will be their protector and refuge. Throughout the psalms, He is described as the defender of the weak and the rescuer of those who call upon His name.

The writer of Psalm 13 clearly believes those promises.

But his experience appears to contradict them.

The problem is not simply that life is difficult. The deeper problem is that the difficulty continues without visible divine intervention.

The psalmist feels forgotten.

The language of the opening verse is remarkably direct:

"How long, O Lord?
Will you forget me forever?
How long will you hide your face from me?"

These words reveal a spiritual wound.

The psalmist does not merely feel sad. He feels abandoned. The God who was expected to be present now appears absent. The God who was expected to respond now appears silent. The God who was expected to act now seems distant.

This is the point where the moral world begins to crack.

If God truly governs the world with justice and compassion, then the faithful should not feel forgotten. If God hears prayer, then cries for help should not disappear into silence.

Yet the psalmist's experience suggests something very different.

The prayers have been spoken.
The waiting continues.
Nothing changes.

This is the first layer of rupture in the psalm.

But the wound goes deeper.

In the second verse, the writer describes what the silence of God does internally:

"How long must I wrestle with my thoughts
and day after day have sorrow in my heart?"

Now the struggle moves inward. The absence of divine response creates a relentless inner battle. The psalmist's thoughts circle around the same questions again and again. Every day brings the same emotional burden.

Anyone who has waited through a long season of unanswered prayer recognizes this experience. The mind begins searching for explanations.

Did I pray incorrectly?
Have I misunderstood God's will?

Is there something wrong with my faith?
Perhaps God is not listening after all.

The longer the silence lasts, the louder those questions become.

This is one of the hidden effects of moral injury in the life of faith. When the moral order of the world appears to break, believers often turn the questions inward. If God is good and the world should make sense, then perhaps the problem must be with me.

The psalmist feels that pressure.

Day after day the thoughts continue. Day after day the sorrow remains. And the silence of God makes the struggle even heavier.

Yet the distress is not only internal.

There is also an external dimension to the rupture.

The second half of verse two introduces another painful reality:

"How long will my enemy triumph over me?"

Now the tension sharpens. Not only does the psalmist feel abandoned by God, but those who oppose him appear to be winning. The enemy's success intensifies the sense that the world is upside down.

In the psalmist's understanding of the moral order, the faithful should ultimately be vindicated while injustice should not prevail.

But what he sees is the opposite.

The enemy triumphs.
The faithful suffer.
God appears silent.

This combination creates the full weight of the rupture. The writer's expectations about God, justice, and the shape of the world have collided with a reality that looks very different.

It is important to notice how the psalmist responds to this tension.

He does not walk away from God.

Instead, he brings the protest directly into prayer. The lament is not spoken behind God's back. It is spoken to God.

This detail matters.

The protest reveals that the relationship with God is still intact. In fact, the lament depends upon that relationship. Only someone who still believes that God hears prayer would cry out with such urgency.

This is why lament plays such a central role in the biblical tradition. Lament allows believers to remain in relationship with God even when the moral order of the world appears broken. Instead of suppressing confusion or pretending that everything makes sense, the psalmist speaks honestly.

"How long, O Lord?"

The question is not polite or restrained. It is urgent, emotional, and repeated four times because the waiting feels unbearable.

And yet the psalm remains a prayer.

This reveals something remarkable about the faith of the psalmist.

The lament assumes that God is still listening.

Even when God feels distant, the psalmist continues speaking to Him.

This is where the moral injury lens helps us see the deeper significance of the passage. Psalm 13 is not simply an emotional complaint. It is a faithful protest in the face of moral disorientation.

The writer believes that God's justice should be visible in the world. When that justice appears delayed, he does not abandon the relationship. Instead, he confronts God with the apparent contradiction.

How long?

The question, in effect, holds God accountable to the expectations created by His own character.

You are just.
You are faithful.
You hear the cries of your people.
So how long will this continue?

This kind of prayer may feel uncomfortable for modern believers. Many Christians have been taught that questioning God reflects weak faith. They assume that proper prayer should always sound calm, confident, and composed.

But Scripture repeatedly gives us a different model.

The lament psalms show that faith can include protest. Faith can include confusion. Faith can include the cry of someone who feels forgotten.

In fact, the willingness to bring such cries before God may be one of the deepest forms of trust.

The psalmist believes that God is big enough to hear the complaint, that the relationship is strong enough to hold the tension, and that the God who seems silent now will eventually respond.

That expectation prepares us for the final movement of the psalm. After speaking honestly about the rupture, the psalmist begins to move toward trust.

But that movement does not erase the lament.

Instead, it shows how faith can survive even in a world where the silence of God feels painfully long.

WHAT THE MORAL INJURY LENS REVEALS

When we read Psalm 13 through the lens of moral injury, something important becomes visible that we might otherwise miss.

The psalm is not merely about emotional distress. It is about the collapse of a moral expectation within the life of faith.

The writer believes something deeply about God and the world: that the Lord sees, hears, and responds to the cries of His people. That conviction is not a minor theological detail. It is woven into the story of Scripture from beginning to end.

God hears Israel's cry in Egypt.
God listens to the prayers of the prophets.
God promises to defend the oppressed and rescue those who call upon His name.

Psalm 13 arises from that same theological world.

The psalmist believes those promises. That is why the silence of God feels so disturbing. The experience of unanswered prayer does not simply create sadness; it creates tension between expectation and reality.

If God hears prayer, why does the waiting continue?
If God defends the faithful, why does the enemy seem to triumph?
If God's face shines upon His people, why does it now feel hidden?

This is precisely the kind of rupture the moral injury lens helps us recognize.

Something in the moral order of the world appears to have broken. The psalmist does not abandon belief in God's goodness, but the experience of silence seems to contradict that goodness.

This tension produces the lament.

Without the moral injury lens, we might treat the lament simply as an emotional moment in the psalm. But when we read carefully, we realize that the lament is actually the heart of the prayer. It expresses the crisis created when a believer's understanding of God collides with painful experience.

Psalm 13 therefore becomes a window into the spiritual life of someone whose expectations about God have been shaken.

But the psalm does something even more remarkable.

It shows us that faith can survive this crisis.

In fact, the structure of the psalm reveals a movement that is deeply important for understanding biblical faith.

The prayer begins with protest.

"How long, O Lord?"

The psalmist does not soften the question. He brings the full force of his confusion into the presence of God. This is not polished religious language. It is the cry of someone who feels forgotten.

Yet after voicing the protest, the psalm moves into petition:

"Look on me and answer, Lord my God.
Give light to my eyes, or I will sleep in death,
and my enemy will say, 'I have overcome him'" (verses 3–4).

Now the prayer becomes specific and urgent. The psalmist asks directly for God's intervention. He pleads for God to see, respond, and restore what has been broken.

This movement from protest to petition is significant.

The lament does not lead the writer away from God. It leads him deeper into conversation with God. The believer who cries "How long?" is still speaking to the Lord.

Then, in the final verses, the psalm moves again.

The language shifts from petition to trust:

"But I trust in your unfailing love;
my heart rejoices in your salvation.
I will sing the Lord's praise,
for he has been good to me" (verse 5–6).

This sudden change in tone has puzzled readers for centuries. How can the psalmist move so quickly from anguish to confidence? Nothing in the psalm suggests that the external situation has changed. The enemy still exists. The waiting may still continue.

And yet something within the writer has shifted.

The key lies in the phrase "your unfailing love."

The Hebrew word translated here as "unfailing love" is hesed, one of the richest words in the Old Testament. It refers to God's covenant faithfulness, His steadfast commitment to His people.

The psalmist remembers that even when circumstances appear uncertain, the character of God remains constant.

This is the turning point of the psalm.

The writer does not suddenly discover an explanation for the silence of God. The mystery remains unresolved. What changes is his focus. Instead of measuring God's faithfulness solely by the present moment, he remembers the larger story of God's covenant love.

The world may feel broken now, but the psalmist still believes that God's character is trustworthy.

That conviction allows him to speak words of hope even before the situation improves.

The moral injury lens helps us see the significance of this movement. The psalm does not erase the rupture. It acknowledges it fully. The questions remain real, and the pain of waiting is not dismissed.

But the psalm also reveals that faith does not depend on immediate answers.

Faith rests on the character of God.

This insight is crucial for pastors and congregations alike.

Many believers assume that faith requires emotional certainty. They imagine that strong faith means never questioning God, never expressing confusion, and never feeling abandoned.

Psalm 13 shows something very different.

Faith sometimes cries out.
Faith sometimes wrestles with the silence of heaven.
Faith sometimes asks the same painful question again and again: "How long?"

And yet the psalmist continues speaking to God.

That persistence reveals the deeper nature of biblical faith. Faith is not the absence of questions. It is the refusal to abandon the relationship with God even when the questions remain unanswered.

This is what the moral injury lens reveals so powerfully in Psalm 13.

The lament is not the opposite of faith.

It is an expression of faith wounded but still alive.

The writer refuses to pretend that the world makes sense. At the same time, he refuses to walk away from the God who holds the world together.

This tension between protest and trust forms the heart of the psalm.

And it prepares us to consider one final question.

If Psalm 13 reveals the spiritual struggle created by divine silence, how should that shape the way pastors preach this passage?

HOW THE MORAL INJURY LENS CHANGES THE SERMON

When pastors preach Psalm 13 without recognizing the rupture at the heart of the text, the sermon often moves too quickly toward reassurance.

The preacher may acknowledge that life sometimes feels difficult. The congregation is reminded that believers occasionally struggle with doubt or discouragement. Then the sermon moves toward the closing lines of the psalm and encourages listeners to trust God's love in spite of their circumstances.

The result is a message that sounds encouraging but may feel disconnected from the deeper experience of the psalm.

People sitting in the pews often know that the struggle described in Psalm 13 is more than a brief emotional downturn. Many believers have lived through seasons when the silence of God lasted far longer than they expected. They have prayed sincerely and waited faithfully, yet the situation remained unresolved.

When sermons move too quickly past the lament, those listeners may feel that their experience has not truly been acknowledged.

The moral injury lens changes the sermon because it refuses to rush past the rupture.

Instead, the preacher recognizes that the psalm gives voice to a genuine crisis of faith: the experience of believing in a just and attentive God while feeling forgotten in the present moment.

Once we see that rupture clearly, the tone of the sermon changes.

The sermon becomes more honest.

Instead of minimizing the tension in the text, the preacher allows the congregation to feel it. The repeated question "How long?" is not softened or explained away. It is heard in its full weight.

People who have prayed through long seasons of silence recognize themselves in the psalmist's words. They realize that Scripture understands the experience they have struggled to describe.

The moral injury lens also deepens the theological dimension of the sermon.

Without this perspective, Psalm 13 might be treated primarily as a lesson about managing difficult emotions. But when we recognize the rupture in the text, we see that the psalm is wrestling with a profound theological question:

What happens when the expectations created by faith collide with the experience of divine silence?

That question is not merely emotional. It concerns the character of God and the shape of the world.

The psalmist believes that God is attentive to His people. When that attentiveness seems absent, the believer must wrestle with the tension between what is believed and what is experienced.

A sermon shaped by the moral injury lens therefore takes the congregation into that tension rather than avoiding it.

The preacher acknowledges that there are seasons when God feels silent. There are moments when prayer seems unanswered. There are situations where the faithful wait longer than they ever expected.

Instead of offering quick explanations, the sermon allows the congregation to hear the honesty of the psalmist's cry:

"How long, O Lord?"

This kind of preaching creates space for wounded faith.

Some people in the congregation may have been carrying that same question silently for years. They may have wondered whether it was acceptable to bring such thoughts into prayer. Hearing the psalm proclaimed honestly reassures them that Scripture itself gives voice to that struggle.

The moral injury lens also changes the direction of hope in the sermon.

Without this perspective, the preacher might imply that the psalmist's confidence at the end comes from discovering an answer or seeing the situation improve.

But the text suggests something different.

Nothing in the psalm indicates that the external circumstances have changed. The enemy still exists. The waiting may still continue. The silence of God may not yet be broken.

What changes is the psalmist's remembrance of God's character.

"But I trust in your unfailing love."

The turning point comes not from a new explanation but from remembering the covenant faithfulness of God. The psalmist's hope rests in the steadfast love that has defined God's relationship with His people throughout the story of Scripture.

This is where the sermon can offer genuine hope without denying the reality of suffering.

The preacher does not pretend that the silence of God always ends quickly. Nor does the sermon attempt to explain every season of waiting.

Instead, it points the congregation toward the deeper foundation of faith: the character of God Himself.

Even when the moral world appears uncertain, the covenant love of God remains constant.

The moral injury lens therefore reshapes the sermon in several important ways.

First, it validates lament. The preacher acknowledges that faithful people sometimes feel forgotten and that Scripture itself gives voice to that cry.

Second, it resists simplistic explanations. The sermon does not attempt to resolve divine silence with easy answers.

Third, it proclaims hope grounded in God's character rather than in immediate circumstances. The psalmist's trust rests in the unfailing love of the Lord, not in the quick resolution of the problem.

Finally, this approach prepares the congregation for the larger story of Scripture.

Psalm 13 teaches believers how to pray when God seems silent. But the biblical story moves toward an even more profound moment of divine silence.

At the cross, Jesus Himself cries out words that echo the language of lament:

"My God, my God, why have you forsaken me?" (Matt 27:46; Ps 22:1).

That cry reveals that the experience of divine silence is not foreign to the story of redemption. Even the Son of God entered the depths of human abandonment.

And yet the story did not end there.

The resurrection reveals that the silence of God is not the final word.

When pastors preach Psalm 13 through the lens of moral injury, they help congregations see that faith can endure even when answers do not come quickly.

The psalm teaches believers how to remain in conversation with God during long seasons of waiting.

The cry "How long?" becomes not a sign of unbelief but an act of trust, a refusal to stop praying to the God whose unfailing love ultimately holds the world together.

SERMON - HOW LONG, O LORD?

Scripture: Psalm 13

There are seasons in the life of faith when the hardest part is not the pain itself. The hardest part is how long the pain lasts. A person can endure much when there is some sign that the end is near, some indication that relief is coming, some evidence that God is moving. But when the days stretch into weeks and the weeks into months, and nothing seems to change, a different kind of struggle begins to emerge. The suffering is still there, but now it is joined by something else. It is joined by waiting. It is joined by uncertainty. It is joined by the terrible quietness that settles over the soul when heaven seems silent.

That is the world of Psalm 13.

This is not the prayer of someone who has just encountered trouble. This is the prayer of someone who has been in trouble long enough for the waiting itself to become part of the wound. The psalmist is not merely hurting. He is hurting while God seems silent. He is praying, but nothing appears to change. He is calling out, but he feels no visible answer. And so the prayer begins with a question that believers have carried in their hearts for generations:

"How long, O Lord?"

That question is one of the most honest questions in all of Scripture. It does not pretend. It does not dress itself up in polished religious language. It does not skip quickly to reassurance. It says what so many faithful people have wanted to say but were afraid to put into words. How long will this continue? How long must I wait? How long will the pain remain? How long will God seem distant? How long will the faithful cry out while nothing changes?

Psalm 13 gives us permission to ask that question.

That matters because many believers have quietly assumed that real faith should sound more composed than this. We imagine that mature prayer should always be steady, calm, and confident. We think that if we are truly trusting God, we should not sound desperate. But the Bible does not present faith that way. The Bible gives us prayers that tremble. It gives us prayers that protest. It gives us prayers spoken through tears. It gives us prayers like this one.

The psalmist cries, "How long, O Lord? Will you forget me forever? How long will you hide your face from me?" Those are not small words. They are bold words. They come from someone who feels not merely troubled but forgotten. The psalmist does not say, "I am having a difficult week." He says, "It feels as though God has turned away."

That is a painful thing to admit. There are believers sitting in churches every week who know exactly what that feels like. They have prayed for healing and the diagnosis has not changed. They have prayed for their marriage and the distance remains. They have prayed for a son or daughter who has wandered far from God, and year after year there is still no sign of return. They have prayed about injustice in the world, about violence in their communities, about grief in their homes, and they have watched the days pass with no clear answer. At some point the hardest part is no longer just the original pain. The hardest part is the silence.

Psalm 13 enters that silence and speaks from within it.

The psalmist goes on: "How long must I wrestle with my thoughts and day after day have sorrow in my heart?" Now the prayer moves from the silence of heaven to the turmoil within. Anyone who has lived in prolonged uncertainty knows this struggle. The mind will not rest. It circles the same questions again and again. Did I do something wrong? Am I praying the wrong way? Is God displeased with me? Have I misunderstood what faith is? Has God heard me at all? Day after day the thoughts return, and day after day the sorrow remains.

The psalmist is not only speaking about external suffering. He is speaking about the inner exhaustion that comes when waiting stretches on too long. The soul becomes tired. The heart becomes heavy. The mind becomes restless. What began as a problem in the world becomes a battle within the self.

Then the psalmist adds one more layer: "How long will my enemy triumph over me?" Now we see that this is not simply private discouragement. There is opposition. There is pressure. There is something wrong not only inside the psalmist but around him. And the worst part is that the opposition seems to be winning. The enemy appears strong. The faithful appear weak. God appears silent.

That is why this psalm feels so morally unsettling. The problem is not just pain. The problem is that the world does not seem to be working the way it should. The faithful cry out, but God seems hidden. The sorrowful pray, but heaven seems quiet. The enemy advances, but justice seems delayed.

This is why the question "How long?" is deeper than frustration. It is a question about the moral order of the world. The psalmist believes that God hears prayer. He believes that God is just. He believes that God cares for His people. He believes that God does not forget the faithful. But his present experience seems to contradict all of that. The result is not simply sadness. It is disorientation.

There are many people in the life of the church who live in that disorientation. They still believe in God, but they no longer know how to make sense of their experience. They still pray, but they feel as though their prayers strike the ceiling and fall back down. They still come to worship, but inside they carry the same exhausted question: How long?

Psalm 13 matters because it does not tell those people to hide that question. It teaches them to pray it.

That is one of the most remarkable things about the psalm. The lament is not spoken to friends about God. It is spoken directly to God. "How long, O Lord?" The protest is still prayer. The confusion is still addressed to the Lord. The pain is still brought into the relationship.

That means the psalmist has not abandoned faith. In fact, this cry is itself an act of faith. Only someone who still believes God hears can pray like this. Only someone who still believes that God matters can protest His seeming absence. Only someone who still believes that God is just can be wounded by the delay of justice.

This is important because many Christians assume that questioning God means they have failed spiritually. They think that if they feel forgotten, if they admit confusion, if they dare to say that God seems silent, then something must be wrong with their faith. Psalm 13 says otherwise. Psalm 13 teaches us that faith does not require pretending. Faith does not require denying the pain. Faith does not require covering the wound with religious language.

Faith can cry out.

Faith can ask why.

Faith can ask how long.

Faith can pray through the silence without yet seeing the answer.

That does not make the silence easier. The psalm does not minimize how painful it is to feel that God has hidden His face. In the Old Testament, the face of God is the sign of divine presence and favor. When God's face shines upon His people, there is blessing, protection, and peace. So when the psalmist cries, "How long will you hide your face from me?" he is speaking from a place of profound spiritual distress. He feels as though the presence he most needs is the presence he cannot perceive.

There are believers who know that feeling very well. They do not doubt God in theory. They simply cannot find Him in the place where they most expected Him to be. They look for Him in the hospital room, in the grieving house, in the long season of unanswered prayer, in the struggle that refuses to end. And in that moment the old promises feel far away. They do not know how to reconcile what they believe about God with what they are experiencing in the present.

This is why Psalm 13 is so merciful. It does not scold the wounded for feeling wounded. It does not rush them into cheerful declarations. It allows the question to be asked. It allows the pain to be named. It allows the confusion to remain visible.

But the psalm does not end there.

After the repeated cry of "How long?" the prayer shifts: "Look on me and answer, Lord my God. Give light to my eyes, or I will sleep in death, and my enemy will say, 'I have overcome him.'" The psalmist moves from protest to petition. He asks God to see him. He asks God to answer. He asks God to intervene.

That movement matters. The pain has not vanished, and the waiting has not yet ended, but the psalmist is still turning toward God. He has not shut down. He has not walked away. He has not decided that prayer is useless. He continues speaking. He continues asking. He continues pleading.

There is deep wisdom here for the life of faith. Many people imagine that unanswered prayer should lead to one of two outcomes: either confident trust or complete collapse. But the psalms show us a third path. They show us the path of honest persistence. They show us a person who does not understand, does not see, does not yet receive, but still speaks to God.

This may be one of the most faithful acts a person can offer in a long season of silence: not polished certainty, but continued prayer.

And then Psalm 13 does something astonishing. Without telling us that the situation has changed, without announcing that the enemy has been defeated, without reporting that the silence has been broken, the psalmist says, “But I trust in your unfailing love; my heart rejoices in your salvation. I will sing the Lord’s praise, for he has been good to me.”

How can he say that?

Nothing in the psalm suggests that the external circumstances have improved. The enemy still exists. The waiting may still continue. The sense of silence may not yet be fully resolved. And yet the psalmist speaks words of trust.

The answer lies in that phrase: “your unfailing love.”

The psalmist turns from the uncertainty of the present moment to the steadiness of God’s character. He does not suddenly understand everything. He does not solve the mystery of the delay. He remembers who God is.

That is where hope enters the psalm.

Not through explanation.

Not through immediate resolution.

But through remembrance.

The psalmist remembers that the Lord’s love is steadfast. He remembers that God’s covenant faithfulness is deeper than the present darkness. He remembers that even when the world feels unstable, the character of God remains unchanged.

This is not denial. It is not shallow optimism. The psalmist has not forgotten the sorrow of the earlier verses. He has carried those verses straight into this final confession. The trust at the end of the psalm is meaningful precisely because it rises from within the struggle, not apart from it.

This is the kind of hope Scripture offers to wounded faith. It is not the hope of quick answers. It is not the hope of easy explanations. It is the hope that rests in the character of God even when the reasons remain hidden.

There are people who need that kind of hope. They do not need to be told that the waiting is easy. They do not need to be given thin answers that explain away their grief. They need to know that faith can survive inside the question. They need to know that trust can still exist while the heart is still aching. They need to know that God's love is not cancelled by His silence.

Psalm 13 teaches us that the life of faith includes both protest and trust. The psalmist does not choose one or the other. He brings both into the presence of God. He protests because he believes God is just. He trusts because he believes God is faithful. He does not yet see the resolution, but he refuses to abandon the relationship.

That is a word the church needs.

There are many people who think they must wait until they feel spiritually strong before they can pray honestly. Psalm 13 says no. Bring the weakness. Bring the confusion. Bring the tiredness. Bring the question. Bring the ache of having waited too long. Bring the wound of heaven's silence. Bring it all to God.

And bring it as prayer.

Because that is what this psalm is. It is not a record of unbelief. It is a prayer spoken by wounded faith. It is the cry of someone who feels forgotten but still speaks to the Lord. It is the language of a believer who cannot make sense of the world but refuses to let go of the God who made it.

And that means Psalm 13 also points us forward.

It prepares us for another cry in Scripture, another prayer spoken from the depths of anguish. At the cross, Jesus Himself cries out, "My God, my God, why have you forsaken me?" The language of lament reaches its deepest point there. The righteous one suffers. The innocent one is condemned. The Son prays, and the darkness remains.

If there were ever a moment when the moral order of the world appeared broken, it was there.

And yet the cross was not the end of the story.

The resurrection tells us that the silence of God is not the final word. The delay is not the end of the story. The hidden face of God is not the last truth about reality. There is a greater truth beneath the silence: the steadfast love of God still holds.

That does not erase the pain of waiting. It does not make every unanswered prayer easy to bear. It does not turn lament into something unnecessary. But it does mean that the faithful can continue to pray, continue to hope, continue to cry out "How long?" without losing their place in the presence of God.

So perhaps that is where this psalm meets us today.

Some of us are still at the beginning of the psalm. We are asking the question with all the weight of our sorrow. How long, O Lord? How long will this continue? How long will the silence remain? How long will the enemy seem strong? How long will the heart keep hurting? If that is where you are, Psalm 13 tells you that your prayer belongs in Scripture. Your cry belongs in the life of faith. You do not need to hide it.

Some of us may be somewhere in the middle of the psalm, still asking God to look, answer, and intervene. We are not yet able to sing, but we are still able to ask. Psalm 13 tells you that this too is faith. Petition is faith. Pleading is faith. Continuing the conversation with God is faith.

And some of us may be able, even through tears, to say the final words: "But I trust in your unfailing love." Not because everything has been resolved, but because we remember who God is. Not because we fully understand the waiting, but because we know the One to whom we are waiting belongs.

The miracle of Psalm 13 is not that it eliminates the question.

The miracle is that it teaches the faithful how to live inside the question.

It teaches us that the silence of God can be brought into the presence of God. It teaches us that lament is not a failure of faith but one of its most honest forms. It teaches us that trust is not the denial of pain but the decision to remember God's steadfast love in the middle of pain.

And so when the silence feels long, when the waiting feels heavy, when the heart grows tired and the enemy seems strong, the church is given words to pray.

How long, O Lord?

And by the grace of God, even that cry can become an act of trust.

Chapter 6

The Cry of Abandonment

Text: Psalm 22

OPENING PASTORAL SCENARIO: WHEN HEAVEN IS QUIET

There are seasons in the life of faith when the hardest part of suffering is not the pain itself. The hardest part is the silence.

Pastors encounter this struggle more often than many people expect. A believer sits in the office describing months of prayer that seem to have produced no answer. Someone cries out to God during a crisis, yet the situation remains unchanged. A person who once felt close to God now speaks about prayer as something that feels empty.

Eventually the words come.

"I feel like God isn't there anymore."

Sometimes people say it cautiously, almost apologetically, as though the thought itself might be inappropriate. Yet beneath the hesitation lies a painful question that refuses to disappear.

Where is God?

The experience of divine silence can be one of the most unsettling moments in the life of faith. It challenges assumptions that many believers carry quietly within them. We assume that prayer will produce some sense of response. We expect that God will feel near during seasons of suffering. We believe that faithfulness will be accompanied by some sign of divine presence.

When those expectations remain unmet, the silence can feel overwhelming.

Scripture does not ignore this experience.

In fact, the Bible preserves a prayer that gives voice to the very feeling many believers struggle to articulate. It appears in Psalm 22, a lament that begins with one of the most famous cries in all of Scripture:

"My God, my God, why have you forsaken me?"

These words are striking because they do not resemble the kind of prayer many people expect to find in the Bible. They are not calm or carefully composed theological reflections. They are the raw cry of someone who feels abandoned.

Yet this prayer appears in the worship book of Israel.

For centuries faithful believers sang these words as part of their relationship with God.

The psalm continues:

"Why are you so far from saving me,
so far from my cries of anguish?" (verse 1).

The speaker is not questioning whether God exists. The question is why God seems absent. The distance between expectation and experience has become unbearable.

God is believed to be near.

Yet God feels far away.

This tension lies at the heart of Psalm 22.

The psalm gives voice to believers who continue praying even when the heavens appear silent. It acknowledges that faith sometimes involves long seasons in which the presence of God feels hidden.

For many modern readers this honesty can be surprising.

We often imagine biblical faith as confident and unwavering. We picture believers speaking with certainty about God's actions and purposes. Yet the Psalms reveal something more complex. They show believers wrestling with confusion, crying out in protest, and asking questions that sound shocking in their intensity.

Psalm 22 stands among the most powerful examples of this tradition.

The writer begins by describing the painful experience of divine distance. He cries out during the day and again during the night, yet the silence continues. The prayers rise repeatedly, but no answer seems to come.

Anyone who has prayed through a long season of uncertainty recognizes this feeling. Prayer begins to resemble a one-sided conversation.

The believer speaks.

The silence continues.

Yet even in these opening verses the psalm reveals something crucial about the nature of faith.

The writer continues speaking to God.

"My God… my God…"

Those words reveal that the relationship has not ended. Even when God seems absent, the psalmist still addresses Him directly. The lament is spoken not about God but to God. The believer refuses to abandon the conversation.

This is one of the most important features of biblical lament.

Faith does not disappear when questions arise. Faith continues praying even when answers do not come quickly.

Psalm 22 represents the next stage in the story we have been tracing through Scripture. Earlier we encountered Psalm 13, where the psalmist repeatedly asked, "How long, O Lord?" That psalm described the experience of waiting for God's intervention while facing opposition and sorrow.

Psalm 22 moves deeper into the experience of divine silence.

The writer no longer asks merely how long the waiting will last. Now the question becomes more painful:

Why does God seem absent at all?

The moral expectations that shaped the psalmist's faith appear to be breaking apart. God is believed to hear the cries of the faithful, yet the cries continue unanswered.

This is where the moral injury lens becomes especially helpful.

The deepest wound in Psalm 22 is not simply suffering. It is the tension between what the psalmist believes about God and what he experiences in the present moment.

God should hear.
God should act.
God should be near.

Yet the silence continues.

The psalm therefore gives voice to one of the most profound struggles in the life of faith:

How do believers continue trusting God when He seems absent?

The answer to that question unfolds throughout the rest of the psalm. Before exploring that movement toward hope, however, we must consider how this passage is usually interpreted and why many sermons move too quickly past the painful tension contained in its opening words.

THE PASSAGE AS WE USUALLY PREACH IT

When Psalm 22 appears in a sermon, the interpretation almost always moves quickly to the cross.

The opening line of the psalm—"My God, my God, why have you forsaken me?"—is quoted by Jesus while He is dying on the cross. Because of that connection, preachers often approach Psalm 22 primarily as a prophetic description of the crucifixion.

The sermon typically highlights the parallels between the psalm and the events recorded in the Gospels. The mockery of enemies, the piercing of hands and feet, and the casting of lots for clothing all seem to anticipate details of Jesus' suffering. These connections are striking, and they understandably draw the attention of readers.

From that perspective, Psalm 22 becomes a remarkable example of prophecy fulfilled.

The preacher then moves toward a familiar conclusion. The psalm points forward to Christ. Jesus fulfills the suffering described in the text. Therefore Psalm 22 ultimately testifies to the redemptive work of the cross.

There is truth in that interpretation. The New Testament itself invites readers to see the connection. When Jesus quotes the opening words of the psalm, He intentionally directs attention to the passage. Early Christians recognized that the language of Psalm 22 echoes many elements of the crucifixion story.

Yet there is a subtle danger when sermons move too quickly in that direction.

When Psalm 22 is treated only as a prediction about Jesus, the original experience behind the psalm can easily disappear from view. The psalm existed for centuries before the crucifixion. For generations it functioned as a prayer within the worship life of Israel.

Faithful people prayed these words.

They sang them in the temple.

They used them to express their own experiences of suffering before God.

In other words, Psalm 22 first existed as the voice of a believer wrestling with the silence of heaven. The psalmist was not writing a theological forecast about a future Messiah. The psalmist was praying in the middle of an experience that seemed impossible to reconcile with what he believed about God.

If we move too quickly to the New Testament fulfillment, we risk missing the pastoral power of the psalm itself. The text becomes a piece of theological information rather than a living prayer spoken from within suffering.

There is another common way Psalm 22 is preached as well.

Many sermons emphasize the ending of the psalm more than its beginning. The final portion of Psalm 22 moves toward praise and confidence. The psalmist begins to declare that God has heard his cry and that future generations will proclaim the Lord's righteousness.

Because of that ending, the psalm is sometimes presented as a quick movement from despair to triumph. The message becomes something like this: the psalmist felt abandoned for a moment, but ultimately everything worked out.

While that interpretation highlights an important dimension of the psalm, it can unintentionally minimize the depth of the struggle described in the opening verses.

The first half of Psalm 22 is not brief or mild. It is a sustained cry of anguish. The psalmist describes humiliation, exhaustion, and isolation. Enemies surround him. His body grows weak. His prayers appear unanswered.

Most painfully, the psalmist feels that God Himself is distant.

"My God, my God, why have you forsaken me?"

These words are not rhetorical decoration. They are the honest expression of someone who cannot reconcile his experience with what he believes about God.

The psalmist knows the stories of God's faithfulness. He remembers how God delivered Israel in the past. The ancestors trusted God, and God rescued them. They cried out, and the Lord answered.

Yet the psalmist's present experience does not match those memories.

He cries out.

And the silence continues.

This contrast between remembered faithfulness and present silence lies at the heart of the psalm. The psalmist knows what God has done before, which makes the current silence even more difficult to understand.

When sermons move too quickly toward resolution—either by jumping directly to the crucifixion or by focusing primarily on the psalm's ending—the tension that drives the entire prayer can easily disappear.

But Psalm 22 invites us to remain inside that tension for a while.

It gives voice to the painful space where prayer continues but answers seem delayed.

It allows believers to speak openly about the experience of divine absence.

This honesty is not a weakness in biblical faith.

It is one of its deepest strengths.

THE MORAL INJURY QUESTION

At this point we return to the diagnostic question guiding our reading:

Where does the moral world appear to break in this passage?

Psalm 22 provides one of the clearest answers to that question anywhere in Scripture. The psalmist is not simply describing suffering; he is confronting a rupture in the expectations that shaped his faith.

The covenant story taught Israel that God hears the cries of His people. Again and again the Scriptures describe God responding to those cries. When Israel suffered in Egypt, God heard their groaning and delivered them. When the people cried out in the wilderness, God provided for them. When the nation faced enemies, God raised up leaders to rescue them.

These stories formed the foundation of Israel's trust.

God hears.
God acts.
God delivers.

Psalm 22 reveals what happens when a believer who trusts that story experiences something very different.

The psalmist cries out repeatedly, yet the expected response does not come.

"O my God, I cry by day, but you do not answer,
and by night, but I find no rest" (verse 2).

The prayer is constant. The writer cries out during the day and continues through the night. Yet heaven remains silent.

The psalmist cannot reconcile that silence with what he knows about God. Immediately after describing the unanswered prayers, he recalls the history of God's faithfulness:

"In you our ancestors trusted;
they trusted, and you delivered them.
To you they cried, and were saved" (verses 4–5).

The contrast is painful.

The ancestors trusted, and God delivered them.

The psalmist trusts, yet the silence remains.

The moral logic of the world appears broken. The relationship between God's character and the events of the present moment no longer seems clear.

Psalm 22 gives voice to this rupture without attempting to hide it.

The psalmist describes humiliation and isolation. Enemies mock him and question his trust in God:

"He trusts in the Lord; let him deliver him" (verse 8).

This mockery deepens the crisis. The silence of God becomes evidence, in the eyes of the enemies, that the psalmist's faith is misplaced.

This is precisely the moment when many believers today feel their faith most deeply challenged. When suffering continues and answers do not appear, people begin to wonder whether their expectations about God were misguided.

Psalm 22 allows that tension to be spoken.

"My God, my God, why have you forsaken me?"

The question is not the abandonment of faith. It is the expression of faith under pressure. The psalmist still addresses God directly, even while questioning His absence.

That detail is crucial.

The rupture has not destroyed the relationship with God. Instead, it has forced the psalmist to bring his deepest confusion into the presence of God.

This is the power of biblical lament.

The believer refuses to remain silent about the tension between belief and experience.

He names it.

He speaks it.

He prays it.

WHAT THE MORAL INJURY LENS REVEALS

Once we recognize the rupture within Psalm 22, the entire psalm begins to look different. What first appears to be a complaint about suffering becomes a prayer spoken from inside a crisis of faith.

The psalmist believes deeply in the character of God. God is holy. God has acted in the past. The history of Israel is filled with stories of divine deliverance.

Yet the present experience contradicts those convictions.

Prayer goes unanswered. Enemies mock the believer's trust. God appears distant.

Psalm 22 is written from inside that tension.

The writer does not stand outside the struggle offering reflection. He is living within it. This is why the language of the psalm is so vivid. Enemies are described as animals—bulls, lions, and dogs—closing in on the sufferer. The imagery communicates vulnerability and danger.

Yet the most striking feature of the psalm is the movement between protest and memory.

Again and again the psalmist shifts between describing present suffering and recalling God's past faithfulness.

After crying out about abandonment, the writer declares:

"Yet you are holy, enthroned on the praises of Israel" (verse 3).

The pattern repeats throughout the psalm. The writer laments the silence of God, then remembers how God delivered the ancestors. He describes humiliation, then reflects on the trust that began even at birth.

These memories do not remove the tension. Instead they intensify it. The psalmist remembers what God has done, which makes the present silence even harder to understand.

This movement reveals something profound about biblical faith.

The psalmist does not abandon belief in God's faithfulness, even while struggling with God's apparent absence.

Both realities are held together.

Faith remembers the character of God.

Experience raises painful questions.

Psalm 22 refuses to simplify this tension. It allows both voices to speak.

Eventually the tone begins to change. The psalmist anticipates the possibility that God will intervene. The language moves gradually from despair toward praise.

The final section of the psalm envisions a future in which the nations proclaim the righteousness of God. Generations yet unborn will hear the story of the Lord's deliverance.

Hope emerges.

But it does not appear by denying the rupture.

Hope emerges because the psalmist brings the rupture into conversation with God.

The believer does not pretend the world still makes sense. Instead he prays through the confusion until a new vision of God's faithfulness becomes possible.

HOW THE MORAL INJURY LENS CHANGES THE SERMON

Recognizing the rupture within Psalm 22 changes the way the passage is preached. The psalm is no longer treated as a quick movement from suffering to victory or simply as a prophecy of the crucifixion. Instead it becomes a window into one of the deepest struggles of faith: what happens when God seems absent.

This recognition changes the tone of the sermon.

Preachers often move quickly toward reassurance, emphasizing the hopeful ending of the psalm. Yet many listeners are living inside the tension the psalm describes. Their prayers have not yet reached resolution.

The moral injury lens slows the sermon down.

Instead of rushing past the cry of abandonment, the preacher lingers with it. Scripture itself contains prayers spoken from within divine silence. The congregation hears that the experience of God's distance is not a failure of faith but part of the biblical story.

This honesty deepens the pastoral impact of the sermon. People who have struggled quietly with unanswered prayer realize that Scripture understands their experience.

The moral injury lens also deepens the theological significance of the text. Psalm 22 becomes part of a larger biblical conversation about suffering and faith.

The psalm connects with Job's protest, with the prophets' laments, and with the cries of those who struggled to understand God's ways throughout Scripture.

Most significantly, the psalm connects with the cross.

When Jesus cries out from the cross using the opening words of Psalm 22, He enters into the same tradition of lament. The cross represents the moment when the moral structure of the world appears most profoundly broken. The innocent sufferer is condemned while injustice triumphs.

Yet the psalm does not end in despair.

And neither does the story of the cross.

When pastors preach Psalm 22 through this lens, the congregation hears a deeper truth about faith. Faith is not destroyed by unanswered prayer. Faith continues praying.

Faith refuses to abandon the relationship with God even when the answers are delayed.

And ultimately faith discovers that God remains present even in moments when His presence seems hidden.

In the sermon that follows, we will see how this passage can be proclaimed in a way that honors the honesty of lament while still pointing the congregation toward the hope that emerges through the story of God's faithfulness.

SERMON: THE CRY OF ABANDONMENT

Text: Psalm 22

There are moments in the life of faith when the hardest part of suffering is not the pain itself but the silence that surrounds it. People often expect suffering to hurt, but they do not expect heaven to feel quiet while it happens. The crisis of faith frequently begins not when life becomes difficult but when prayer seems to disappear into silence.

Pastors hear this struggle more often than people realize. A believer sits in the office describing months of prayer that seem to have produced no answer. Someone cries out to God during a crisis, yet the situation remains unchanged. A person who once felt close to God now says that prayer feels empty, as if the conversation that once felt alive now echoes without reply.

Eventually the words come.

Sometimes they are spoken slowly and carefully, as though the person is unsure whether it is acceptable to say them out loud. Sometimes they are spoken through tears. But beneath the hesitation is the same question that has echoed through generations of believers.

Where is God?

The experience of divine silence can be deeply unsettling for people of faith because it seems to contradict what they believe about God. Christians believe that God hears prayer. They believe that God cares about His people and draws near to them in their suffering. They believe that the Lord is attentive to those who call upon His name.

When those expectations collide with the experience of silence, something inside the believer begins to feel disoriented. Prayer continues, but answers do not appear. Faith remains, but the sense of God's presence feels distant. The believer continues to speak, yet heaven seems quiet.

Psalm 22 gives voice to that experience.

The psalm opens with one of the most famous cries in the entire Bible: "My God, my God, why have you forsaken me?" These words are striking because they sound so raw and unfiltered. They are not the kind of carefully composed religious language that many people expect to find in Scripture. Instead, they sound like the anguished cry of someone who feels abandoned.

Yet these words appear in the worship book of Israel.

For centuries faithful believers sang this psalm as part of their prayers. The people of God included these words in their worship because they recognized that the experience described in the psalm was not foreign to the life of faith. There are moments when believers feel that God is distant, and Psalm 22 gives them language for those moments.

The psalm continues with a description of relentless prayer: "O my God, I cry by day, but you do not answer, and by night, but I find no rest." The psalmist is not describing a brief moment of discouragement but a prolonged season of unanswered prayer. The writer cries out during the day and continues through the night, yet the silence remains.

Anyone who has prayed through a long season of uncertainty recognizes this experience. The prayers continue, but the answers seem delayed. The believer keeps speaking to God, yet the sense of response never quite appears.

What makes this psalm even more powerful is that the writer knows the stories of God's faithfulness. The psalmist remembers how God delivered Israel in the past. The ancestors trusted God, and God rescued them. They cried out, and the Lord answered.

The psalmist says, "In you our ancestors trusted; they trusted, and you delivered them." Those memories make the present silence even more painful.

The psalmist knows that God has acted in the past, and that knowledge intensifies the confusion of the present moment.

If God answered them, why does He seem silent now?

This tension lies at the heart of the psalm. The writer believes deeply in the character of God, yet the present experience seems to contradict that belief. The moral expectations that shaped the psalmist's faith appear to be breaking apart.

God should hear.

God should act.

God should be near.

Yet the silence continues.

Psalm 22 gives believers permission to speak honestly about that tension. The psalmist does not hide his confusion or pretend that everything makes sense. Instead, he brings his deepest questions directly to God.

"My God, my God, why have you forsaken me?"

This question is not spoken about God but to God. The psalmist refuses to abandon the relationship even while questioning what is happening within it. The believer continues speaking to the Lord, even when the answers do not appear.

This is one of the most important features of biblical lament. Faith does not disappear when questions arise. Faith continues praying even when the prayers seem unanswered.

Many people assume that strong faith means never questioning God, but the Psalms tell a different story. Again and again Scripture shows believers crying out with confusion, frustration, and longing. These prayers are not signs of weak faith but expressions of faith under pressure.

The psalmist continues to pray because the relationship with God still matters.

Psalm 22 also describes the social dimension of suffering. The writer is surrounded by enemies who mock his trust in God. They say, "He trusts in the Lord; let him deliver him." Their words turn the silence of God into a weapon. If God truly cared about this person, they argue, surely God would intervene.

Anyone who has suffered publicly knows how painful this experience can be. When life falls apart, people often interpret suffering as evidence that something must be wrong with the person who is suffering. The silence of God becomes, in the eyes of observers, proof that faith has failed.

The psalmist refuses to accept that interpretation. Instead, he continues to cry out to God even while surrounded by voices that question his trust.

As the psalm unfolds, the language becomes vivid and intense. The writer describes enemies surrounding him like animals—bulls, lions, and dogs closing in on their prey. The imagery communicates vulnerability and exposure. The psalmist feels overwhelmed by forces beyond his control.

Yet even in the middle of this distress, something remarkable happens. The psalmist continues to remember the faithfulness of God. After crying out about abandonment, the writer declares, "Yet you are holy, enthroned on the praises of Israel."

This movement between protest and memory appears throughout the psalm. The writer describes suffering, then recalls the faithfulness of God in the past. The psalmist laments the silence of heaven, then remembers the stories of deliverance that shaped the faith of Israel.

These memories do not remove the tension. Instead, they intensify it. The psalmist remembers what God has done before, which makes the present silence even harder to understand.

But the psalmist refuses to let go of either reality.

The pain remains real.

The memory of God's faithfulness remains real.

Both truths exist together within the prayer.

This is the kind of faith Psalm 22 describes. It is not a faith that denies suffering or pretends that everything makes sense. It is a faith that continues speaking to God even when the world feels confusing.

This psalm became even more powerful centuries later when its opening words appeared again at a moment of unimaginable suffering. As Jesus hung on the cross, He cried out, "My God, my God, why have you forsaken me?"

With those words Jesus reached back into the language of Psalm 22. The Son of God entered fully into the cry of abandonment that the psalmist had spoken generations earlier.

At the cross the moral structure of the world appears completely broken. The innocent sufferer is condemned while injustice triumphs. The Messiah is mocked by those who watch Him die. The one who trusted perfectly in God experiences the anguish described in this psalm.

Yet Jesus does not speak these words as an act of despair. He speaks them as a prayer.

Even in the darkest moment of suffering, Jesus continues to address God as "My God." The relationship remains intact even when the experience of abandonment feels overwhelming.

This connection between Psalm 22 and the cross reveals something extraordinary about the story of the gospel. The experience described in this psalm is not merely the struggle of an ancient believer recorded in Israel's hymnbook. It becomes part of the story of Christ Himself.

God does not remain distant from the experience of divine silence.

God enters it.

Jesus experiences the depth of human suffering and the anguish of feeling abandoned. He enters the place where many believers fear they are alone.

Yet the story of the cross does not end in abandonment.

Psalm 22 itself does not end in despair either. As the psalm moves forward, the tone begins to shift. The writer starts to anticipate the possibility that God will intervene. The language gradually moves from lament toward hope.

The final section of the psalm describes a future in which the nations proclaim the righteousness of God. The psalmist envisions generations yet unborn hearing the story of the Lord's deliverance.

Hope emerges from within the prayer.

It does not appear by denying the suffering or pretending that the silence never happened. Instead, hope grows out of the persistent conversation between the believer and God.

The psalmist continues praying until a new vision of God's faithfulness becomes possible.

The story of Jesus follows the same pattern. The cross represents the deepest moment of suffering and apparent abandonment, yet it is not the end of the story. Three days later the silence of the tomb is broken by resurrection.

The resurrection declares that the silence of God is never the final word.

For believers today, Psalm 22 offers both honesty and hope. The psalm reminds us that faith sometimes involves seasons when God feels distant. Prayer can continue for long periods without visible answers. The experience of divine silence is not a failure of faith but part of the reality of life in a broken world.

At the same time, the psalm teaches believers how to live within that silence. The psalmist does not abandon the conversation with God. Instead, the believer continues praying.

Faith refuses to stop speaking to God even when heaven seems quiet.

The story of the cross assures us that God understands this experience from the inside. Jesus entered the depth of human suffering and spoke the words of this psalm from the cross. Because of that, no believer ever cries out in abandonment alone.

The God who seems silent is the same God who entered our suffering and carried it to the cross.

And the God who entered that suffering is the same God who raised Jesus from the dead.

For that reason, the cry of Psalm 22 does not lead ultimately to despair. It becomes part of a larger story in which suffering is real, silence can feel overwhelming, but God's faithfulness remains deeper than both.

The believer may not always see how the story will unfold. The answers to prayer may not appear as quickly as we hope. Yet faith continues praying because the relationship with God endures even in the silence.

"My God… my God…"

Those words remind us that the conversation with God never truly ends.

And because the resurrection stands at the center of the Christian story, believers can trust that even when heaven seems quiet, God is still at work in ways we cannot yet see.

Chapter 7

Faith After the World Ends

Text: Lamentations 3

OPENING PASTORAL SCENARIO: WHEN A WORLD COLLAPSES

There are moments in life when suffering feels like a chapter.

And there are moments when suffering feels like the end of the whole story.

A family loses their home in a fire. A community is shattered by violence. A nation experiences war or disaster that leaves entire neighborhoods in ruins. Individuals sometimes walk through tragedies so severe that the life they once knew seems gone forever.

In pastoral ministry these moments appear more often than we might expect. A person sits across from a pastor and says something like this:

"I don't know how to move forward. Everything that made life feel stable is gone."

It may be the death of a spouse after decades of marriage. It may be the loss of a career that defined a person's identity. It may be the collapse of a family through betrayal or separation.

Whatever the cause, the experience feels the same.

The world as it once existed has ended.

The Bible has language for moments like this. It speaks not simply of difficulty but of catastrophe, the collapse of an entire moral and social world. Few books of Scripture capture this experience as vividly as Lamentations.

Lamentations was written after one of the most devastating events in Israel's history: the destruction of Jerusalem in 586 BC. The city had stood at the center of Israel's life for centuries. It was the location of the temple, the place where the people believed the presence of God dwelt among them. It was the political and spiritual heart of the nation.

And then it was destroyed.

The Babylonian army surrounded Jerusalem, breached its walls, burned the temple, and carried many of the people into exile. This event did not simply change Israel's political situation. It shattered the entire framework through which the people understood their relationship with God.

The temple was gone.

The monarchy had collapsed.

The land promised to their ancestors was now controlled by a foreign empire.

For generations the people had believed that Jerusalem stood under God's protection. The covenant promises seemed to assure them that the city would endure. When destruction came, it felt as though the moral order of the world had collapsed.

Lamentations is the voice of people standing in the ruins.

The book is composed of poems that express grief, confusion, and spiritual disorientation. The writers do not rush toward explanations or reassurance. Instead, they describe the devastation with painful honesty.

Jerusalem, once full of life, now sits empty. The streets are silent. The temple is a smoldering ruin. The people are scattered and broken.

This is not merely a national tragedy.

It is a theological crisis.

If God was present in the temple, what does its destruction mean? If God promised to protect His people, why did this catastrophe happen? If the covenant defined the moral structure of Israel's world, what happens when that structure collapses?

The writers of Lamentations do not avoid those questions.

They bring them into prayer.

This moment in Scripture represents an important step in the story we have been tracing throughout this book. Earlier we encountered individuals wrestling with moral rupture. Abraham faced an unimaginable command that challenged his understanding of God. Job struggled with the suffering of the innocent. The psalmists cried out when God seemed silent.

Now the crisis becomes communal.

An entire nation experiences moral injury at the same time.

The people who once believed they lived within the protection of God now stand amid ruins wondering how faith can survive. The old world, the one that seemed morally coherent and divinely ordered, has collapsed.

And yet Lamentations does something remarkable.

It continues speaking to God.

The poems are filled with sorrow and protest, but they remain prayers. The writers do not abandon the relationship with God even while wrestling with the catastrophe that has overtaken them.

This persistence reveals something profound about biblical faith.

Faith is not limited to moments when life makes sense. It does not depend on circumstances that feel stable or predictable. Faith can survive even when the world that once seemed secure has fallen apart.

Lamentations teaches believers how to speak to God after the world ends.

This is why the book remains so relevant for modern readers. Every generation encounters moments when the stability of life disappears. Communities experience disasters. Nations face violence and upheaval. Individuals suffer losses that feel overwhelming.

When those moments come, the question rises again:

How do we live faithfully when the world we knew is gone?

Lamentations does not answer that question quickly. Instead, it invites us to stand for a moment within the ruins. It allows us to see the devastation honestly before moving toward hope.

The passage we will focus on in this chapter comes from the center of the book, Lamentations 3. This chapter contains some of the most familiar words in Scripture:

"Because of the Lord's great love we are not consumed,
for his compassions never fail.
They are new every morning;
great is your faithfulness" (verses 22–23).

These words have been sung in hymns and quoted in sermons for generations. They are beautiful expressions of hope.

But to understand their power, we must first remember where they appear.

They are spoken in the middle of catastrophe.

The city still lies in ruins. The suffering has not ended. The people are still living with the consequences of destruction. Yet in the midst of that devastation, a voice begins to speak about the steadfast love of God.

The journey toward that hope begins in the darkness of grief.

In the next section we will explore how this passage from Lamentations is usually preached and why familiar interpretations sometimes overlook the depth of the rupture that produced these words.

THE PASSAGE AS WE USUALLY PREACH IT

When Lamentations 3 appears in sermons, the focus almost always falls on one particular portion of the chapter. Many Christians recognize the words immediately:

"Because of the Lord's great love we are not consumed,
for his compassions never fail.
They are new every morning;
great is your faithfulness."

These verses have been sung in hymns for generations. They appear in devotionals, prayer guides, and funeral services. They are often quoted in moments when believers need encouragement or reassurance.

And rightly so.

They are beautiful words.

The passage speaks about God's compassion, His faithfulness, and the renewal of mercy with each new day. In a world that often feels unstable, those promises bring comfort. As a result, sermons on Lamentations 3 frequently emphasize God's faithfulness in difficult times. The preacher reminds the congregation that even when life becomes painful, God's mercies are new every morning.

There is truth in that message. The text does proclaim the faithfulness of God, and the declaration "Great is your faithfulness" expresses a profound confidence in the character of the Lord.

But something important is often lost when the passage is preached this way.

Many sermons treat these verses almost as though they stand independently from the rest of the chapter. The surrounding context receives only brief attention before the sermon moves quickly to the hopeful lines about God's mercy.

Yet the structure of Lamentations 3 suggests something very different.

The declaration of God's faithfulness does not appear at the beginning of the chapter. It emerges from the middle of a long and painful reflection on suffering.

The writer opens the chapter with a series of striking images that describe life under the weight of catastrophe:

"I am the one who has seen affliction
by the rod of the Lord's wrath.
He has driven me away and made me walk
in darkness rather than light" (verses 1–2).

The tone of these lines is very different from the verses usually quoted in sermons. The speaker describes feeling surrounded by darkness, trapped behind walls, and burdened by grief. The language conveys the experience of someone who believes that God Himself has allowed the suffering to continue.

The chapter continues with imagery of exhaustion and despair. The writer speaks of prayers that seem blocked, paths that appear twisted, and hope that feels distant.

One of the most painful lines appears a few verses later:

"So I say, 'My splendor is gone
and all that I had hoped from the Lord'" (verse 18).

This is not a passing moment of discouragement.

It is the voice of someone who believes that the world as they knew it has collapsed.

When sermons focus only on the hopeful verses in the middle of the chapter, this darker section can easily be overlooked. But the lament is not a minor introduction to the passage. It is the environment from which the declaration of hope emerges.

The writer is not speaking about God's faithfulness from a place of comfort or stability.

He is speaking from within devastation.

The city of Jerusalem has been destroyed. The temple lies in ruins. The people have been displaced from their homes. Everything that once defined the identity of the community has been shattered.

The writer of Lamentations stands amid those ruins.

That context changes the way we hear the famous lines about God's mercy.

Without recognizing the depth of the catastrophe, we might interpret the passage as a simple reminder that God is faithful during ordinary hardship. But the writer is describing something far more severe.

The entire moral and spiritual world of the community has collapsed.

For generations the people believed that Jerusalem stood under God's protection. The temple symbolized the presence of the Lord among His people. The covenant promises seemed to assure them that their relationship with God would endure.

Yet now the temple has been burned.

The city has fallen.

The people have been scattered.

From a human perspective, the covenant world appears shattered.

This is why the opening section of Lamentations 3 is filled with such intense language. The writer is trying to describe what it feels like to live through a catastrophe that seems to contradict everything the people believed about God's relationship with them.

The grief is not only emotional.

It is theological.

The people are struggling to understand how their faith can survive when the structures that once supported it have disappeared.

When we overlook this context, the familiar verses about God's mercy can sound almost like inspirational slogans. They become general statements about optimism rather than hard-won declarations spoken from the depths of suffering.

But when we read the entire chapter carefully, we realize that the writer is doing something far more courageous.

He is affirming God's faithfulness after the world has fallen apart.

The words "Great is your faithfulness" do not come from someone living in stability. They come from someone who has seen everything collapse and still dares to believe that God's compassion has not ended.

This perspective changes the way the passage should be preached.

Instead of presenting these verses as simple encouragement, the sermon must acknowledge the devastation that surrounds them. The hope of Lamentations 3 is powerful precisely because it rises from within catastrophe.

The writer is not ignoring the ruins.

He is standing in them.

And from that place he begins to speak about the mercy of God.

Understanding this context prepares us to ask the central diagnostic question that guides our reading throughout this book.

Where does the moral world appear to break in this passage?

When we ask that question of Lamentations 3, the depth of the crisis becomes unmistakable.

THE MORAL INJURY QUESTION: WHERE DOES THE MORAL WORLD BREAK?

At this point in each chapter we pause and ask the diagnostic question that helps us read Scripture through the lens of moral injury:

Where does the moral world appear to break in this passage?

In Lamentations 3 the answer is not subtle.

The rupture is everywhere.

The entire book exists because the moral world of Israel appears to have collapsed.

For generations the people of Israel believed that their lives were anchored in a covenant relationship with God. That covenant shaped how they understood history, justice, and the structure of the world. The temple symbolized the presence of God among the people. The monarchy represented the continuation of God's promises. The land itself was the visible sign that God had fulfilled His covenant with their ancestors.

Together these realities created a sense of moral coherence.

The people believed they lived within a world governed by God's justice and faithfulness. Even when difficulties arose, the covenant promises provided assurance that God remained present and attentive.

But the destruction of Jerusalem shattered that world.

The Babylonian invasion did more than defeat an army or conquer a city. It dismantled the visible framework through which Israel understood its relationship with God.

The temple was burned.

The walls of Jerusalem were broken down.

The Davidic monarchy collapsed.

Large portions of the population were taken into exile.

From a human perspective, everything that symbolized God's covenant presence had been destroyed.

This is the moment where the moral world appears to break.

If God dwells in the temple, what does it mean when the temple is gone?

If God protects His people, why has their city fallen?

If the covenant promises stability, why does the community now stand in ruins?

The writers of Lamentations do not avoid these questions. They describe the devastation with painful honesty.

Throughout the book we hear images of a once-thriving city now sitting empty. The streets that once echoed with celebration are silent. The temple that once hosted worship now lies in ashes.

In chapter 3 the writer describes the experience in deeply personal language:

"I am the one who has seen affliction
by the rod of the Lord's wrath.
He has driven me away and made me walk
in darkness rather than light."

The speaker feels surrounded by suffering.

God, who once guided His people with light, now seems to have placed them in darkness. The writer even describes feeling trapped behind walls with no way out. The imagery suggests confinement, exhaustion, and a sense that every path forward has been blocked.

At one point the writer says something that reveals the depth of the rupture:

"So I say, 'My splendor is gone
and all that I had hoped from the Lord.'"

That sentence captures the emotional and theological crisis of the moment.

The hope that once defined the people's faith now feels distant. The structures that supported their understanding of God's presence have been removed. The world they believed in appears to have collapsed.

This is precisely the kind of moment the moral injury lens helps us recognize.

Moral injury occurs when deeply held expectations about justice, goodness, or divine faithfulness are violently disrupted by experience. The people of Israel believed that the covenant relationship with God defined the moral structure of their world. When Jerusalem fell, that structure seemed to disintegrate.

The suffering they experienced was not merely physical or political.

It was spiritual.

The people were forced to confront the possibility that the world no longer operated according to the expectations they had trusted for generations.

This is why the language of Lamentations is so intense.

The writers are not merely documenting historical events. They are trying to articulate the spiritual disorientation that follows the collapse of a moral world.

They describe hunger, grief, humiliation, and fear. They speak of broken hearts and shattered hopes. They acknowledge that the catastrophe has left them struggling to understand the relationship between God and history.

Yet something remarkable happens within the chapter.

Even while describing the collapse of their world, the writer continues speaking to God.

This is not a detached reflection on suffering.

It is a prayer rising from within the ruins.

The writer does not abandon the relationship with God. Instead he brings the confusion directly into conversation with the Lord. The lament becomes a form of spiritual honesty.

This is one of the most important insights the moral injury lens reveals in Scripture.

The Bible does not pretend that catastrophic suffering leaves faith untouched. It acknowledges that moments of devastation create deep spiritual wounds. They shake assumptions, challenge expectations, and force believers to reconsider how they understand the world.

But the biblical response to that rupture is not silence.

It is lament.

Lament allows the wounded community to continue speaking to God even when the moral structure of life feels broken. It creates space for grief, protest, and confusion within the life of faith.

Lamentations 3 therefore stands as a powerful example of how Scripture gives voice to moral injury.

The writer does not deny the devastation of Jerusalem. He does not pretend that the catastrophe makes sense. Instead, he speaks honestly about the suffering while continuing to address God directly.

This persistence reveals something profound about biblical faith.

Faith does not disappear when the moral world breaks.

Faith continues speaking to God from within the ruins.

And it is precisely within that conversation that something unexpected begins to emerge.

In the middle of this chapter, after describing the depth of suffering, the writer begins to speak about the steadfast love of the Lord.

Those words do not erase the devastation around him.

But they reveal that even after the collapse of a world, the story of God and His people is not over.

In the next section we will explore what becomes visible in the passage when we recognize this rupture clearly.

WHAT THE MORAL INJURY LENS REVEALS

When we read Lamentations 3 through the lens of moral injury, we begin to see something that is easy to miss when the passage is quoted in isolation.

The famous declaration about God's faithfulness does not arise from comfort.

It rises from catastrophe.

The writer of Lamentations is not reflecting on God's goodness during an ordinary hardship. He is speaking from within the collapse of his entire world. The temple has been destroyed. The city lies in ruins. The covenant community has been scattered. Everything that once symbolized stability and divine presence appears to have vanished.

And yet, in the middle of this devastation, the writer says something remarkable:

"Yet this I call to mind
and therefore I have hope" (verse 21).

The word "yet" marks a turning point in the chapter. It signals a deliberate shift. The writer does not deny the suffering that surrounds him. The ruins of Jerusalem are still visible. The grief of the people remains real. But he begins to recall something deeper than the catastrophe.

He remembers the character of God.

"Because of the Lord's great love we are not consumed,
for his compassions never fail.
They are new every morning;
great is your faithfulness" (verse 22–23).

When we hear these words through the moral injury lens, their significance becomes clearer.

The writer is not claiming that life has returned to normal. The city has not been rebuilt. The people have not yet been restored. The suffering of exile still lies ahead.

Instead, he is making a declaration about something that survived the collapse of the world he once knew.

The character of God has not changed.

The covenant structures that once defined Israel's life have been shattered. The temple is gone. The monarchy has fallen. The land has been lost. But the steadfast love of God remains.

This is the theological breakthrough at the center of Lamentations 3.

The people of Israel had long understood the presence of God through visible institutions. The temple symbolized the dwelling place of the Lord. The monarchy represented the continuation of divine promises. The land embodied the covenant relationship between God and His people.

When those institutions collapsed, it seemed as though the covenant itself had failed.

But the writer of Lamentations begins to realize that God's faithfulness does not depend on those structures. Even when the visible signs of the covenant disappear, the character of God remains unchanged.

His compassion does not fail.

His mercy does not run out.

His faithfulness continues from one generation to the next.

The writer expresses this realization through a phrase that has echoed through centuries of worship: "They are new every morning."

These words do not mean that suffering disappears overnight. The writer still stands in the ruins of Jerusalem when he speaks them. Instead, the phrase points to the daily renewal of God's mercy even within a devastated world.

Every morning the sun rises again.

Every morning life continues.

Every morning the possibility of grace remains.

This insight transforms the writer's perspective.

Earlier in the chapter he described feeling trapped in darkness, surrounded by walls, and burdened by sorrow. He even confessed that the hope he once had in the Lord seemed to have vanished.

But now he begins to see that the catastrophe has not destroyed the most important reality of all.

God's steadfast love still holds the story together.

The moral injury lens helps us understand how profound this realization truly is.

When the moral structure of the world collapses, people often feel that everything has been lost. The assumptions that once guided life no longer seem reliable. The systems that once provided meaning appear broken.

In those moments it is easy to believe that the story has ended.

The writer of Lamentations initially feels that same despair. The devastation of Jerusalem seems to confirm that the covenant world has collapsed beyond repair.

Yet he discovers something unexpected within the ruins.

The covenant was never sustained by buildings or political power alone.

It was sustained by the character of God.

The temple may be destroyed, but God's compassion is not destroyed.

The monarchy may have fallen, but God's faithfulness has not fallen.

The land may be occupied by foreign armies, but God's mercy still rises with each new morning.

This realization does not erase the suffering of the present moment. The writer does not pretend that the devastation has suddenly disappeared. Instead, he learns to anchor hope in something deeper than the visible structures that once defined the world.

He anchors hope in God Himself.

This shift reveals one of the most important lessons of the entire book of Lamentations.

Faith can survive the collapse of a world.

The destruction of Jerusalem felt like the end of everything the people knew. Yet even in that moment the covenant relationship with God continued. The people still had a God who heard their cries, remembered His promises, and extended mercy beyond the ruins.

This discovery prepares the way for the future story of Israel.

The exile would not be the end of the covenant. The people would eventually return to their land. The city would be rebuilt. Worship would resume in a restored temple.

But even more important than those future events is the theological insight that emerges in Lamentations.

The faithfulness of God is not confined to a single place or institution.

God remains faithful even when the visible signs of His presence appear to vanish.

For pastors and congregations today, this insight speaks directly into moments of deep loss. Individuals sometimes experience personal catastrophes that feel like the end of the world they once knew. Communities face tragedies that shatter the structures that once sustained them.

In those moments the temptation is to believe that everything has been lost.

Lamentations 3 invites us to see something different.

Even when the world collapses, the character of God remains constant.

His compassion still rises with each morning.

His faithfulness still holds the story together.

Recognizing this truth prepares us to ask the final question for this chapter.

If Lamentations 3 reveals that hope can emerge from within the ruins, how should that shape the way pastors preach this passage?

In the next section we will explore how the moral injury lens transforms the sermon itself, helping congregations hear the power of these words in the midst of their own broken worlds.

HOW THE MORAL INJURY LENS CHANGES THE SERMON

When pastors preach Lamentations 3 without recognizing the rupture that surrounds the passage, the sermon often becomes a simple message about encouragement.

The preacher quotes the familiar lines:

"Because of the Lord's great love we are not consumed...
great is your faithfulness."

The congregation hears a reminder that God's mercy is renewed every morning. The sermon encourages believers to trust that God remains faithful even during difficult times.

There is truth in that message. God's compassion does renew each day. His faithfulness does not fade with changing circumstances. For generations Christians have drawn strength from these words.

But when the passage is preached without acknowledging the devastation that surrounds it, something essential is lost.

The power of Lamentations 3 does not come from optimism.

It comes from the fact that these words are spoken after the world has collapsed.

The writer is not reflecting on God's goodness during an ordinary hardship. He is speaking from within one of the greatest catastrophes in Israel's history. The temple has been destroyed. The city lies in ruins. The people have been displaced from their homes.

Everything that once seemed stable has disappeared.

When we recognize that context, the declaration of God's faithfulness becomes far more powerful. The writer is not ignoring the devastation.

He is standing in the middle of it.

A sermon shaped by the moral injury lens begins by acknowledging that reality.

Instead of starting with reassurance, the preacher allows the congregation to feel the weight of the catastrophe. The sermon describes the ruined city, the shattered hopes of the people, and the theological confusion that followed the destruction of Jerusalem.

The congregation begins to see that Lamentations is not a gentle devotional reflection.

It is the voice of people standing in the ashes of their world.

This honesty changes the tone of the sermon.

Rather than offering quick encouragement, the preacher invites listeners to recognize how faith can survive moments when everything appears lost. The lament becomes part of the message rather than an uncomfortable prelude that must be rushed past.

Many people sitting in the pews know what it feels like to stand in the ruins of their own lives.

Some have lost loved ones in ways that still feel unreal. Others have watched careers collapse, families fracture, or communities change in painful ways. Some carry memories of disasters, violence, or tragedies that altered their sense of safety forever.

For those listeners, the language of Lamentations is not abstract poetry.

It is familiar ground.

When a sermon acknowledges the depth of that experience, the congregation realizes that Scripture understands their pain. The Bible does not pretend that life always unfolds in orderly ways. It contains prayers and poems written by people who faced devastation and struggled to understand how faith could survive it.

The moral injury lens therefore allows the preacher to speak honestly about catastrophe.

It gives permission to name the moments when the moral world appears to collapse. It allows the sermon to acknowledge that there are seasons when the old frameworks that once sustained faith no longer seem reliable.

But the sermon does not remain in the ruins.

Lamentations 3 also reveals something extraordinary about hope.

The writer does not discover hope because the catastrophe has ended. The city is still destroyed. The exile still lies ahead. Nothing about the external circumstances has improved.

Yet the writer remembers something deeper.

"The Lord's great love."

This phrase becomes the turning point of the chapter. The writer realizes that although the visible structures of the covenant world have collapsed, the character of God remains unchanged.

God's compassion has not failed.

God's mercy continues.

God's faithfulness still holds the story together.

A sermon shaped by the moral injury lens therefore points the congregation toward this deeper foundation of hope.

Instead of promising that life will quickly return to normal, the preacher proclaims that God's steadfast love remains present even when the world has fallen apart. The hope of Lamentations 3 is not rooted in restored circumstances but in the unchanging character of God.

This distinction is crucial for pastoral ministry.

When sermons promise that suffering will soon resolve itself, people who continue to struggle may feel that their faith has somehow failed. But when hope is grounded in God's character rather than in immediate outcomes, believers discover that faith can endure even through long seasons of devastation.

The moral injury lens also connects this passage to the broader story of Scripture.

The destruction of Jerusalem once seemed like the end of Israel's story. Yet the biblical narrative continued beyond the ruins. The people would eventually return from exile. The temple would be rebuilt. The covenant story would move forward in unexpected ways.

Most importantly, the faithfulness of God would ultimately be revealed in the coming of Christ.

Jesus entered a world still marked by the consequences of exile and suffering. The people of Israel continued to live under foreign rule. The longing for restoration remained strong.

In that world Jesus proclaimed the kingdom of God and demonstrated the compassion of the Father. Yet the story reached its own moment of catastrophic rupture when the Messiah Himself was crucified.

At the cross it appeared once again that the moral world had collapsed.

The one who embodied God's justice and mercy was executed by the powers of the world. For the disciples, the crucifixion felt like the destruction of everything they had hoped for.

But the story did not end there.

The resurrection revealed that even the deepest catastrophe cannot overcome the faithfulness of God. The same steadfast love described in Lamentations ultimately triumphed over death itself.

This is why the message of Lamentations remains so powerful.

The writer standing in the ruins of Jerusalem could not yet see the full shape of God's redemption. Yet he discovered the truth that would carry the people of God through generations of suffering: the compassion of the Lord never fails.

Every morning His mercy appears again.

A sermon shaped by this insight becomes deeply pastoral.

It speaks honestly about the moments when the world collapses. It acknowledges the grief of people who feel surrounded by ruins. But it also proclaims that even in those moments the story of God's faithfulness continues.

The mercy of God rises with every morning.

His compassion does not run out.

And even after the world ends, His faithfulness remains.

SERMON - FAITH AFTER THE WORLD ENDS

Scripture: Lamentations 3

There are some seasons of suffering that feel like a hard chapter in life. They are painful, disruptive, and exhausting, but they still feel like part of a story that will eventually continue in a recognizable way. A person loses a job, but another opportunity may come. A season of illness passes. A strained relationship begins to heal. The pain is real, but life still feels somewhat intact.

Then there are other moments when suffering does not feel like a chapter at all. It feels like the end of the whole world.

A marriage collapses after decades of trust. A spouse dies, and the house grows so quiet that even ordinary routines begin to feel foreign. A family loses its home in a fire and stands in the driveway looking at ashes where a life once stood. A community is shattered by violence. A nation is broken by war, exile, or disaster. In those moments people do not simply say, "This is hard." They say, "I do not know who I am anymore. I do not know what comes next. Everything that made life feel stable is gone."

That is the world of Lamentations.

Lamentations is not a book written from the middle of an ordinary hardship. It is written from the ruins of catastrophe. Jerusalem has fallen. The temple has been burned. The walls are broken. The people are scattered. The city that once stood at the center of Israel's life now lies in ashes. The place where the people believed God's presence dwelled among them has been destroyed.

That matters because Jerusalem was not just a city. It was the center of a whole way of seeing the world. The temple symbolized the presence of God. The monarchy symbolized the continuation of God's promises. The land symbolized the covenant faithfulness of the Lord. These were not small things. They were the visible structures that held Israel's world together.

And then they were gone.

So Lamentations is the language of people standing in the wreckage, trying to understand how faith can survive after the world they knew has ended. It is the speech of people who cannot return to normal because normal no longer exists. It is grief spoken from inside a collapsed world.

That is why Lamentations 3 begins where it does. "I am the one who has seen affliction by the rod of the Lord's wrath. He has driven me away and made me walk in darkness rather than light." These are not mild words. The speaker is not describing inconvenience. He is describing devastation. He feels driven into darkness. He feels hemmed in. He feels crushed under grief. He feels as though every path forward has been blocked.

That kind of language may seem uncomfortable in church because it sounds too raw, too direct, too honest. But Scripture gives us this chapter because God knows there are moments when anything less than this kind of honesty would be false. There are experiences that cannot be addressed with cheerful slogans. There are losses so deep that the soul cannot skip quickly to reassurance. There are ruins that must first be named as ruins.

And some of you know what that feels like.

Some of you have stood in a moment where the old life ended and the new life had not yet begun. Some of you have watched a future you counted on disappear in a single phone call, a diagnosis, a betrayal, a funeral, a disaster, or a collapse you never imagined would come. Some of you know what it means to look around at the pieces of a life and say, "I do not know how to move forward from here."

Lamentations is written for people like that.

It is written for the person who does not need shallow optimism but truthful faith. It is written for the believer who still speaks to God, even while standing in the ashes. It is written for those who cannot pretend that the world still makes sense.

This chapter is especially important because it does not begin with hope. That is not because hope is absent from Scripture. It is because biblical hope is not sentimental. It does not arrive by denying the catastrophe. It arrives only after the catastrophe has been seen for what it is.

The writer says, "My splendor is gone and all that I had hoped from the Lord." That is a devastating sentence. The writer is confessing that what once gave shape, beauty, meaning, and expectation to life now feels gone. Hope itself feels damaged. The old certainties have not merely been shaken; they have been shattered.

This is one of the great gifts of the Bible. Scripture tells the truth about what catastrophic suffering does to people. It does not merely wound the emotions. It wounds the imagination. It wounds the sense of meaning. It wounds the framework through which people once understood their lives.

That is why suffering of this kind is not only painful. It is disorienting. It makes the world feel morally unstable. If God is faithful, what happened here? If God is present, what do these ruins mean? If life was supposed to be held together by covenant and mercy and promise, why does everything now look like collapse?

Lamentations does not rush to answer those questions. It lets them breathe. It lets them ache. It lets them remain in the open air of prayer.

And that is an important thing to notice. Lamentations is still prayer.

The writer has not walked away from God. The writer has not concluded that speech is useless. The writer is still speaking, still naming the pain, still bringing the catastrophe into the presence of the Lord. That may not sound like strong faith to some people, but in the Bible it is exactly what faithful people do. They bring the broken world to God. They do not hide the ruins. They pray from within them.

Sometimes the holiest thing a person can do is not to explain the catastrophe but to tell the truth about it before God.

That is what this chapter is doing.

The writer describes bitterness, darkness, affliction, tears, and the loss of hope. He does not speak from a place of emotional distance. He speaks from inside the devastation. And that means when hope finally appears in this chapter, it will not be cheap. It will not be decorative. It will not be the kind of hope that floats above suffering and refuses to touch it.

It will be the kind of hope that rises from the rubble.

That is why the turning point in this chapter is so powerful. After naming the darkness, after confessing the collapse, after telling the truth about what has been lost, the writer says, "Yet this I call to mind and therefore I have hope."

That little word "yet" carries enormous weight.

It does not erase what came before it. It does not deny the affliction, the sorrow, the darkness, or the ruins. It stands in the middle of them. It says, in effect, "All of this is true. The devastation is real. The grief is real. The world I knew has collapsed. Yet there is something else I must remember if I am going to keep living."

Then come the words many believers know by heart: "Because of the Lord's great love we are not consumed, for his compassions never fail. They are new every morning; great is your faithfulness."

Those words are beautiful, but they become even more powerful when we remember where they are spoken.

They are not spoken from comfort.

They are spoken from catastrophe.

They are not spoken after the city has been rebuilt.

They are spoken while the city still lies in ruins.

They are not spoken after all questions have been answered.

They are spoken while the pain is still present.

That changes the way we hear them.

The writer is not saying, "Everything is fine." He is not saying, "The suffering was not so bad after all." He is not saying, "Life has already returned to normal." He is saying something much deeper. He is saying that when the visible world collapses, the character of God has not collapsed with it.

That is the breakthrough.

The temple is gone, but God's compassion is not gone.

The walls are broken, but God's mercy is not broken.

The monarchy has fallen, but God's faithfulness has not fallen.

The city is ashes, but the steadfast love of the Lord has not turned to ashes.

That is what the writer calls to mind.

The hope of Lamentations 3 is not rooted in improved circumstances. It is rooted in the unchanging character of God. The writer discovers that even after the world has ended, the Lord remains who He has always been.

This is why the chapter says, "His compassions never fail." Not, "our institutions never fail." Not, "our plans never fail." Not, "our world never falls apart." The chapter does not deny that many things fail. It has already described those failures in painful detail. What it says is that beneath all the failures of history, beneath the collapse of cities and systems and expectations, there remains one reality that does not fail: the compassion of God.

That is where hope becomes possible.

Not because the writer can rebuild the city by an act of will. Not because the grief has ended. Not because the wounds are no longer open. Hope becomes possible because the story is not ultimately being held together by temples, kings, walls, careers, marriages, homes, or even the visible stability of our world. It is being held together by the mercy of God.

That is what allows the writer to say, "They are new every morning."

This is not the language of denial. It is the language of survival. Morning still comes. The sun still rises. Mercy still meets the shattered people of God one day at a time. The writer is not imagining some grand emotional triumph. He is saying that even in the ruins, the Lord gives enough mercy for the next morning.

And sometimes that is all faith can do.

There are seasons when faith cannot imagine ten years ahead. It cannot rebuild the whole city in one day. It cannot fix what has been broken. It cannot answer every question about why the catastrophe happened. It can only wake up and discover that God's mercy has arrived again for this morning.

That is enough.

Not enough to make the pain disappear.

Not enough to undo the ruin immediately.

But enough to keep the story from ending in despair.

Many people need that kind of hope because their lives do not feel rebuildable all at once. They do not need someone to tell them that everything will be easy. They do not need a sermon that rushes them past their grief. They need to know that when the world has ended, mercy still rises in the morning.

That is what Lamentations gives them.

It gives them permission to grieve honestly.

It gives them language for catastrophe.

And it gives them a form of hope that does not depend on pretending the catastrophe never happened.

This kind of hope is deeply important because many Christians quietly assume that faith should look strong, composed, and steady. They imagine that if they trusted God more fully, they would not feel so disoriented after great loss. But Lamentations tells another story. It tells us that faithful people can stand in ruins and still struggle to understand what God is doing. It tells us that believers can feel shattered and still belong to God. It tells us that lament is not the opposite of faith. It is one of faith's truest languages in a fallen world.

The writer of Lamentations does not reach hope by bypassing grief. He reaches hope by walking through grief, naming it before God, and discovering that the character of God is deeper than the collapse of the world around him.

That is a word the church needs to hear.

Because some people are trying to have faith after the world ended.

Some are trying to pray after the funeral.

Some are trying to trust God after betrayal.

Some are trying to keep living after the diagnosis, the disaster, the collapse, the loss that split life into before and after.

For them, faith may no longer look like certainty. It may look like waking up and breathing a prayer through tears. It may look like opening Scripture with trembling hands. It may look like saying, "I do not understand any of this, but I am still here, and God is still God."

Lamentations says that is real faith.

And this chapter also points us beyond itself. The destruction of Jerusalem felt like the end of Israel's story, but it was not. The people would return from exile. The city would one day be rebuilt. The covenant story would continue. But even those later mercies are not the deepest answer of Scripture.

The deepest answer comes in Christ.

Jesus entered a world still marked by exile, sorrow, and the long memory of ruin. He came into a people who knew what it was to lose a world. He proclaimed the kingdom of God in a land shaped by longing, disappointment, and hope deferred. And then He Himself walked into the greatest catastrophe of all, the cross.

At the cross the disciples experienced their own form of world-ending sorrow. The one in whom they had placed their hope was arrested, condemned, and executed. The future they had imagined seemed destroyed. Once again the moral world appeared to collapse. Once again faith stood amid ruins.

But the resurrection revealed what Lamentations had already begun to teach: catastrophe is not the end of God's faithfulness.

The same steadfast love that met Israel in the ruins of Jerusalem met the disciples at the empty tomb. The same mercy that was new every morning in Lamentations became resurrection life on the first day of the week. The same faithfulness that held the covenant story together through exile and ashes raised Jesus from the dead.

That means the gospel does not tell us that worlds never end.

It tells us that even when they do, God remains faithful.

This is why Christian hope is not fragile optimism. It is not the naive belief that life will always feel stable. It is the settled conviction that the mercy of God survives the collapse of every false security. It rises in the ruins. It speaks in the ashes. It meets us the morning after the worst day we imagined.

So if you are standing in the wreckage of something today, hear the witness of Lamentations.

If the old life is gone, the steadfast love of the Lord is not gone.

If the structures that once made you feel safe have collapsed, the character of God has not collapsed.

If the world you knew has ended, the story of God with you has not ended.

His compassions have not failed.

They are new every morning.

Great is His faithfulness.

Those words are not sentimental. They are defiant. They are spoken by people who have every visible reason to despair and yet dare to remember that God's mercy is larger than their ruin.

And that may be what faith looks like for some of us today.

Not having every answer.

Not feeling instantly restored.

Not pretending that the ruins are not real.

But standing in the middle of devastation and saying, "Yet this I call to mind, and therefore I have hope."

That hope may begin very small. It may be no larger than the next prayer, the next breath, the next morning. But it is real because it does not come from us. It comes from the God whose mercy does not run out.

Faith after the world ends does not begin with rebuilding everything.

It begins by remembering who God is.

And when that remembrance takes root, even in the rubble, hope begins to rise.

PART III

GOD ENTERS THE RUPTURE

Chapter 8

My God, Why Have You Forsaken Me?

Text: Matthew 27:46 / Mark 15:34

OPENING PASTORAL SCENARIO: WHEN FAITH FEELS ABANDONED

There are moments in life when suffering reaches a depth that words struggle to express. In those moments people do not simply feel pain; they feel confusion. Something about the world no longer makes sense. The expectations that once gave life a sense of order seem to collapse all at once.

Pastors encounter these moments regularly. Someone sits quietly across the desk and tries to describe what has happened. The loss of a loved one has shaken their faith. A devastating diagnosis has left them wondering why prayer has not changed the situation. A betrayal or injustice has wounded them in ways they never expected.

At some point the conversation often turns toward a question that many believers hesitate to ask aloud.

Where was God?

The question does not always come with anger. Often it comes with quiet confusion. The person still believes in God. They still want to trust. But their experience seems to contradict what they thought they understood about God's presence and care.

For many believers this moment feels frightening. They worry that asking such a question might reveal weak faith. They assume that faithful people should always feel confident that God is near.

Yet when we turn to Scripture, we discover that the Bible speaks honestly about this struggle.

The Bible does not pretend that faith always feels clear and confident. Instead, it gives voice to moments when believers feel overwhelmed by suffering and confusion. The Psalms include prayers that ask how long God will remain silent. The book of Job records the anguish of a righteous man who cannot understand why he suffers. The prophets lament the destruction of Jerusalem and the apparent collapse of the covenant world.

The Bible does not silence these cries.

It preserves them.

But nowhere does this struggle appear more vividly than at the cross.

In the Gospels of Matthew and Mark we encounter a moment that stands at the very center of the Christian story. As Jesus hangs on the cross, nearing the end of His suffering, He speaks words that echo the language of Psalm 22:

"My God, my God, why have you forsaken me?" (Matt 27:46, Mark 15:34).

These words are among the most haunting sentences in all of Scripture.

They are startling not only because of what they say but because of who speaks them. The voice crying out from the cross is the voice of Jesus Himself, the one who taught His disciples to trust the Father and the one who spoke constantly about God's kingdom and God's presence.

Again and again in the Gospels Jesus describes an intimate relationship with the Father. He prays with confidence. He speaks of God's will with clarity. He encourages others to trust that God knows their needs and hears their prayers.

Yet in this moment we hear Him cry out as though God has abandoned Him.

For many readers this moment raises profound questions.

How can the Son of God speak these words?

What does it mean for Jesus to experience the feeling of abandonment?

What does this moment reveal about the relationship between suffering and faith?

These questions become even more striking when we remember the events that led to the cross.

Jesus' ministry had revealed the compassion and power of God in extraordinary ways. He healed the sick. He welcomed those whom society rejected. He proclaimed good news to the poor and freedom for the oppressed. Crowds gathered around Him because they believed something new was happening through His life and teaching.

Many people believed Jesus was the long-awaited Messiah, the one through whom God would restore Israel and establish His kingdom.

Yet the story now appears to end in a shocking way.

Jesus is arrested by the authorities. His disciples scatter. Religious leaders accuse Him of blasphemy. The Roman governor orders His execution. Soldiers mock Him. Crowds jeer at Him as He hangs on the cross.

From every human perspective, the scene looks like the complete collapse of hope.

The one who proclaimed the kingdom of God now dies under the authority of the Roman Empire.

The one who spoke of God's faithfulness now cries out as though God has abandoned Him.

In that moment the moral logic of the world appears to break apart.

The righteous one suffers.

The innocent one is condemned.

And heaven seems silent.

This moment gathers together many of the themes we have been tracing throughout this book. Again and again Scripture confronts moments when the moral order of the world appears to collapse. The faithful cry out to God when suffering seems undeserved. The righteous struggle to understand why injustice continues.

At the cross those questions reach their most intense expression.

The cry of Jesus does not come from someone standing outside the struggle of faith. It comes from the very center of it.

"My God, my God, why have you forsaken me?"

These words echo the ancient language of lament, yet they also introduce a new and profound dimension to the biblical story. The Son of God enters fully into the experience of abandonment that many believers fear most.

The moral injury lens helps us recognize why this moment matters so deeply. Moral injury occurs when the expectations that shape our understanding of the world appear to collapse. The cross represents the ultimate moment when those expectations seem shattered.

If God is just, why does the righteous one suffer?

If God is faithful, why does the Messiah die?

If God is present, why does heaven appear silent?

These questions echo through the scene at Golgotha.

Yet the Gospels do not avoid them. They record the cry of Jesus openly, allowing readers to feel the full weight of the moment.

Before we can understand what this cry reveals about God's work through the cross, however, we must first consider how this passage is usually interpreted and why many sermons move quickly past the disturbing honesty contained in Jesus' words.

THE PASSAGE AS WE USUALLY PREACH IT

When pastors preach the crucifixion, the focus usually centers on the theological meaning of Christ's death. The sermon often moves quickly toward explaining what the cross accomplishes: atonement for sin, reconciliation with God, and the salvation offered through Christ. These themes are essential to the gospel, and they rightly stand at the center of Christian preaching.

Because those truths are so important, however, something subtle often happens in the way this particular passage is handled. The disturbing cry of Jesus—"My God, my God, why have you forsaken me?"—is sometimes treated as a brief theological problem that must be explained away before moving on to the larger message of redemption.

In many sermons the moment receives only a short explanation. Preachers may say that Jesus quoted Psalm 22 in order to fulfill prophecy, or they may explain that Jesus experienced the separation from God caused by human sin. These explanations are not wrong. Both belong within the Christian understanding of the cross.

But when we move too quickly toward explanation, we sometimes overlook the emotional and spiritual force of the moment itself.

The Gospels present this cry not as a minor detail but as one of the final words spoken by Jesus before His death. Mark's Gospel in particular builds toward this moment with striking intensity. Darkness covers the land. The suffering of Jesus has reached its final stage. Then, in a loud voice, Jesus cries out the opening line of Psalm 22.

The evangelists do not soften the words. They do not reinterpret them for us. They allow the cry to stand exactly as it was spoken.

"My God, my God, why have you forsaken me?"

For many readers this moment feels deeply uncomfortable. It seems to raise questions about Jesus' relationship with the Father that we would rather avoid. Some wonder whether these words suggest doubt or despair. Others struggle to reconcile them with the confidence Jesus expresses throughout the rest of the Gospels.

Because of that discomfort, sermons sometimes move past the cry too quickly. The preacher may explain its meaning in a sentence or two and then hurry toward the resurrection. The focus shifts toward the victory that lies ahead, leaving the moment of abandonment behind as something that must simply be endured on the way to Easter morning.

Yet the Gospel writers do not treat this moment lightly.

They place the cry of Jesus at the center of the crucifixion narrative. It stands as one of the defining features of the scene. The suffering of the cross is not only physical; it is spiritual and relational as well. The one who has lived in perfect communion with the Father now experiences a moment that feels like abandonment.

If we listen carefully to the story, we notice something else. The people standing around the cross misunderstand what is happening. Some think Jesus is calling for Elijah. Others mock Him, assuming that God has truly abandoned Him.

In their eyes, the cross confirms their assumptions about failure.

From their perspective, Jesus' mission has collapsed. The teacher who spoke about God's kingdom now dies powerless before the authorities. The one who healed others cannot save Himself. Even His cry to God appears unanswered.

The scene reveals a world where the moral expectations of justice and faithfulness appear shattered.

This is where the moral injury lens begins to open the passage in a new way.

Instead of treating Jesus' cry as a brief theological puzzle to be explained, the moral injury perspective invites us to recognize the full weight of the moment. Jesus is not simply quoting a psalm as a literary reference. He is entering the language of lament that runs throughout Scripture.

Psalm 22 begins with the same cry of abandonment that Jesus speaks from the cross. The psalmist describes feeling surrounded by enemies, mocked by others, and abandoned by God. Yet the psalm also continues beyond that opening cry, eventually moving toward trust and hope.

By quoting the opening line of Psalm 22, Jesus places His suffering within the larger story of biblical lament.

THE MORAL INJURY QUESTION: WHERE DOES THE MORAL WORLD BREAK?

At this point in the chapter we pause and ask the interpretive question that guides this entire book:

Where does the moral world appear to break in this passage?

This question slows our reading and invites us to notice the tension that exists inside the text itself. Moral injury occurs when the expectations that make the world feel morally coherent suddenly collapse. Something happens that should not happen, and the framework through which we understand reality begins to fracture.

When we apply this question to the scene at the cross, the rupture becomes unmistakable.

The moral order of the world appears to collapse in several ways at once.

First, the righteous suffer.

Throughout Scripture the expectation of moral order is clear. God is just. God defends the innocent. God stands with the oppressed and confronts injustice. Even when suffering appears in the biblical story, there remains an underlying conviction that God ultimately upholds righteousness.

Yet at the cross the most righteous person who has ever lived is condemned and executed. Jesus has done nothing deserving punishment. The Gospels portray Him consistently as one who heals the sick, welcomes the marginalized, and proclaims the mercy of God. Even Pilate recognizes that Jesus has committed no crime worthy of death.

And yet He is crucified.

This is not simply a tragic event. It represents a profound rupture in the moral expectations that shape the biblical story. If the righteous one suffers like this, what does that say about the justice of the world?

Second, injustice appears to triumph.

The authorities who oppose Jesus succeed in their plan. Religious leaders who felt threatened by His teaching persuade the Roman governor to condemn Him. The machinery of imperial power carries out the execution efficiently and publicly.

From every visible perspective, the forces of injustice have won.

The crowd that once followed Jesus now mocks Him. Soldiers gamble for His clothing. Religious leaders stand nearby and taunt Him, suggesting that if He truly trusted God, God should rescue Him now.

Their mockery exposes the moral tension of the moment. They believe the cross proves that Jesus was wrong. If God truly favored Him, surely God would intervene.

Instead, heaven remains silent.

Third, the faithful one feels abandoned.

This may be the most startling element of the scene. Jesus has consistently trusted the Father throughout His ministry. In moments of difficulty He retreats to prayer. In moments of decision He seeks the Father's will. His entire life reflects an unbroken relationship with God.

Yet at the cross He gives voice to the feeling that God has forsaken Him:

"My God, my God, why have you forsaken me?"

The words do not sound like calm theological reflection. They sound like the cry of someone who feels utterly alone.

This moment represents the deepest point of rupture in the biblical story. The Son of God enters fully into the human experience of abandonment.

From the perspective of moral injury, the cross becomes the place where every expectation about how the world should work seems to collapse simultaneously.

The righteous suffer.

Injustice triumphs.

God appears silent.

Faith itself seems shaken.

For many people this mirrors experiences they have faced in their own lives. When tragedy strikes, when injustice persists, when prayers seem unanswered, the world can feel morally disordered. The assumptions that once gave life meaning suddenly feel fragile.

People begin asking questions that sound very much like the cry of Jesus:

Why is this happening?

Where is God?

Has God abandoned us?

The remarkable thing about the Gospels is that they do not hide this moment of tension. They do not edit Jesus' words or soften their impact. The cry of abandonment remains at the center of the story.

This honesty matters deeply for preaching.

Many sermons about the cross move quickly toward explaining what Jesus accomplished through His death. Those explanations are essential to Christian faith, but if we move too quickly past the rupture itself, we risk missing something important.

The cross does not merely solve a theological problem.

It reveals the depth of God's willingness to enter the brokenness of the human world.

At the cross, God does not remain distant from moral collapse.

God enters it.

Jesus stands precisely at the point where faith struggles most. The cry of abandonment reveals that the Son of God does not avoid the experience of moral rupture. He steps directly into it.

Understanding this rupture prepares us to see what the moral injury lens reveals about the meaning of the cross itself.

Because the cross is not only the place where the moral world appears to break.

It is also the place where God enters that brokenness in order to redeem it.

WHAT THE MORAL INJURY LENS REVEALS

Once we recognize the rupture at the center of this passage, something remarkable begins to emerge. The cry of Jesus is no longer simply a theological puzzle that requires explanation. Instead, it becomes a window into the way God responds to the deepest wounds of the human world.

The moral injury lens reveals that the cross is not merely the place where suffering happens.

It is the place where God enters the moment when the moral order of the world appears to collapse.

To see why this matters, we must remember the pattern that runs throughout Scripture. Again and again the biblical story confronts moments when life no longer makes sense. The righteous suffer. The faithful cry out. The moral logic of the covenant appears to break down.

We saw this in Abraham's story when God asked him to sacrifice Isaac. We saw it in the book of Job when a righteous man endured suffering he could not explain. We saw it in the psalms of lament when believers cried out to God in moments of confusion and pain.

In each of those moments the question is essentially the same.

How can we trust God when the world seems morally broken?

The cross brings that question to its most intense point. The expectations that shape the biblical worldview appear to collapse all at once. The Messiah suffers. The innocent is condemned. God appears silent.

If the story ended there, the cross would represent the ultimate defeat of hope.

But the Gospels present the scene differently. They invite us to look again at the cry of Jesus, not as the end of faith but as the place where God enters fully into the human experience of moral rupture.

When Jesus cries out, "My God, my God, why have you forsaken me?" He is not stepping outside the story of God's people. He is stepping directly into it. Those words come from Psalm 22, one of the great lament psalms of the Old Testament.

Psalm 22 begins with the cry of abandonment, but it does not end there. As the psalm continues, the voice of lament gradually moves toward trust. The sufferer remembers God's faithfulness in the past and clings to hope even in the midst of suffering.

By quoting the opening line of that psalm, Jesus places His suffering within the larger tradition of biblical lament.

But something even more profound is happening.

The lament of Psalm 22 originally belonged to a human sufferer who felt abandoned by God. At the cross, those same words come from the lips of the Son of God. The one who shares the very life of God enters the experience of abandonment that human beings fear most.

In other words, God Himself steps into the place where faith feels most fragile.

The cross reveals that God does not redeem the world from a distance. God enters the deepest wounds of the world personally. The cry of Jesus shows us that the Son of God is willing to experience the full weight of human suffering, including the terrifying feeling that God has disappeared.

For those who live with moral injury, this revelation is profound.

Moral injury often leaves people feeling isolated. When the moral order of the world collapses, people begin to wonder whether their experience places them outside the reach of faith.

The cry of Jesus speaks directly into that fear.

The Son of God Himself has stood in the place where faith feels abandoned. He has entered the moment when heaven seems silent. He has spoken the same words that countless believers have whispered through tears:

"My God, why have you forsaken me?"

Because Jesus speaks those words, no human cry of abandonment falls outside the story of redemption.

The cross does not bypass the experience of moral rupture.

It enters it completely.

God does not dismiss the cry of the wounded.

God joins it.

HOW THIS CHANGES THE SERMON

Recognizing the rupture at the center of this passage changes the way pastors preach the cross.

Many sermons about the crucifixion focus primarily on explanation. The preacher explains how Jesus' death atones for sin and reconciles humanity with God. These truths are central to Christian faith and must always remain part of the gospel proclamation.

But when we read the passage through the moral injury lens, we notice something else happening in the text.

Before it explains redemption, it gives voice to human anguish.

The cry of Jesus is the emotional center of the crucifixion narrative. When Jesus cries out, "My God, my God, why have you forsaken me?" the Gospel writers invite us to hear the full depth of that lament.

If we rush past that moment too quickly, we lose the pastoral power of the passage.

People in our congregations often carry experiences that feel very much like the cry of Jesus. They have faced moments when life collapsed unexpectedly. A diagnosis shattered the future they imagined. A relationship ended in betrayal. A tragedy left them wondering how such suffering could exist in a world governed by a good God.

In those moments the world no longer feels morally coherent.

The expectations that once gave life stability suddenly feel fragile. People begin asking questions that sound uncomfortably similar to the cry from the cross.

Where is God?

Why did this happen?

Has God abandoned me?

The moral injury lens invites pastors to preach this passage differently.

Instead of avoiding the cry of abandonment, the sermon allows it to speak. The preacher acknowledges the tension of the moment and names the experience of moral rupture that so many people recognize in their own lives.

When the sermon begins this way, something important happens.

People realize that Scripture understands their struggle. They discover that the Bible does not silence their questions but gives them language. The cry of Jesus assures them that faith does not require pretending the world always makes sense.

Even the Son of God entered the place where life felt unbearable.

This changes the tone of the sermon.

Rather than offering quick answers, the preacher stands with the congregation inside the tension of the text. The sermon becomes a space where lament is permitted and honesty is welcomed.

From that place, hope begins to emerge.

Because the story does not end with the cry of Jesus.

The resurrection will reveal that God was present even in the moment when heaven seemed silent.

But the power of Easter becomes clearer when we first allow ourselves to feel the weight of Good Friday.

The moral injury lens helps us preach the cross in a way that acknowledges the depth of human suffering while still proclaiming the hope of redemption.

Instead of bypassing the cry of Jesus, the sermon lingers there long enough for the congregation to recognize something remarkable.

The Son of God has entered the darkest place of human experience.

He has spoken the words that wounded believers have whispered for generations.

"My God, my God, why have you forsaken me?"

And because He has entered that moment, no cry of abandonment lies outside the reach of God's redemption.

Sermon - "My God, my God, why have you forsaken me?"

Text: Matthew 27:46; Mark 15:34

Those words are among the most haunting sentences in all of Scripture. They come to us from the cross itself, spoken by Jesus in the final hours of His suffering. The Gospels of Matthew and Mark both preserve the cry exactly as it was spoken, allowing us to hear the anguish in the voice of the One who hangs between heaven and earth.

When we read these words we often feel a kind of tension. We know who Jesus is. We confess that He is the Son of God, the one who lived in perfect communion with the Father. Throughout His ministry He spoke with deep confidence about God's presence and God's will. He taught His disciples to pray to the Father and assured people that God knows their needs and hears their prayers.

Yet here, in the darkness of the cross, the same Jesus cries out as though God has abandoned Him.

"My God, my God, why have you forsaken me?"

For many believers this moment feels difficult to understand. We might wonder why the Son of God would speak these words, and we may feel tempted to move quickly past them in order to reach the resurrection. But the Gospel writers do not hurry away from this moment. They place the cry of Jesus at the center of the crucifixion story and allow it to echo through the narrative. If we slow down long enough to listen, we discover that this cry reveals something profound about the heart of the gospel.

To understand why these words matter so deeply, we must remember the scene in which they are spoken. Jesus has already endured betrayal, arrest, and humiliation. His disciples have scattered in fear. The religious authorities have accused Him, and the Roman governor has condemned Him to death. Soldiers have mocked Him and nailed Him to a cross outside the city.

The crowds that once followed Him now stand at a distance. Some watch in sorrow, others in curiosity, and some in open ridicule. The One who proclaimed the kingdom of God now hangs powerless under the authority of Rome. From every visible perspective, the story appears to have ended in failure. This is the moment when Jesus cries out with words that have echoed through the centuries:

"My God, my God, why have you forsaken me?"

These words are not random. They come directly from Psalm 22, one of the great laments of the Old Testament. That psalm begins with the same cry of abandonment. The writer describes feeling surrounded by enemies, mocked by others, and abandoned by God. For generations the people of Israel prayed those words during moments when life no longer made sense. The psalm gave language to believers who felt overwhelmed by suffering and confusion.

Now those same words come from the lips of Jesus.

This detail matters because it tells us something about what Jesus is experiencing at the cross. The Son of God enters the language of lament that runs throughout Scripture. He speaks the same cry that wounded believers have spoken in their darkest moments.

"My God, my God, why have you forsaken me?"

Many people throughout history have whispered similar words during seasons of suffering. A parent standing beside a hospital bed wonders why a child must endure such pain. A family grieving an unexpected loss asks why their prayers seemed unanswered. A person who has experienced betrayal or injustice wonders where God was in the middle of the crisis.

These questions do not arise from unbelief. They arise from faith struggling to understand a world that no longer makes sense. At times life feels morally ordered. We believe that goodness matters, that faithfulness matters, and that God watches over the world with justice and care. Yet sometimes events occur that seem to contradict those expectations, and when they do the moral structure of the world appears to fracture.

The righteous suffer.
Injustice continues.

God seems silent.

This is the place where many believers quietly struggle. They still believe in God and still want to trust Him, but something about their experience has shaken the assumptions that once made faith feel secure.

And that is why the cry of Jesus matters so deeply.

When Jesus speaks these words He is not standing outside the human experience of suffering. He is standing directly inside it. The Son of God enters the place where faith feels fragile and the world appears morally broken. At the cross Jesus experiences the same moment of abandonment that countless believers have feared.

"My God, my God, why have you forsaken me?"

The cross therefore reveals something astonishing about the character of God. God does not redeem the world from a distance. God enters the brokenness of the world personally. The Son of God steps directly into the darkest place of human experience.

Throughout Scripture we see people wrestling with suffering they cannot explain. Job struggled to understand why a righteous man should endure such pain. The psalmists cried out to God when injustice appeared to go unanswered. The prophets lamented the destruction of Jerusalem and the collapse of the covenant world.

In each of those moments the same question rises to the surface.

How can we trust God when the world seems morally broken?

At the cross that question reaches its most intense expression. The righteous one suffers. The innocent is condemned. Heaven appears silent. Yet the one who cries out in that moment is not merely another sufferer.

It is the Son of God Himself.

Jesus enters fully into the experience of abandonment that human beings fear most. He takes upon Himself the place where the world seems to fall apart. This means that no cry of anguish is foreign to the heart of God.

Every question spoken through tears, every moment when faith feels fragile, and every prayer whispered in confusion has already been spoken by Christ Himself.

The cross shows us that God understands the depth of human suffering not only in theory but in experience. Jesus has stood in the place where heaven seems silent. He has spoken the words that wounded believers have whispered for centuries.

"My God, my God, why have you forsaken me?"

This truth changes the way we think about suffering in the life of faith. Sometimes people assume that strong faith means never feeling abandoned by God. They imagine that faithful believers always feel confident and secure. When moments of confusion arise, they begin to worry that something must be wrong with their faith.

But the cry of Jesus shows us something different.

Faith does not mean the absence of questions. Faith sometimes speaks through questions. Faith sometimes cries out in anguish. Faith sometimes stands at the edge of despair and still calls out to God.

Even the Son of God prayed with words that sounded like confusion and pain.

"My God, my God, why have you forsaken me?"

Yet there is something else happening in this cry that we must not overlook. Even in the moment of abandonment, Jesus continues to address God.

"My God."

The words are spoken twice.

"My God, my God."

That detail reveals something important. Even in the darkness of the cross, Jesus does not abandon the relationship with the Father. He continues speaking to God. The lament is not spoken about God; it is spoken to God.

That is one of the most important features of biblical lament. The person who feels abandoned by God still speaks to God. The relationship is strained and painful, but it is not abandoned.

Jesus continues praying even when heaven seems silent.

This is why the cry of the cross can become a prayer for believers today. There are seasons when faith feels steady and confident, when prayer flows easily and the presence of God feels near. But there are also seasons when life becomes confusing and the answers we hoped for do not appear.

In those moments the cry of Jesus reminds us that we are not alone.

The Son of God has already stood in that place. He has already spoken those words.

"My God, my God, why have you forsaken me?"

But the story does not end there.

The cross appears to be the final collapse of hope, yet the Gospels tell us that another chapter follows. The silence of Good Friday is eventually broken by the dawn of Easter morning.

The resurrection reveals that God was present even in the moment that appeared most empty of hope.

What looked like abandonment was not the end of the story.

It was the place where God was accomplishing the deepest work of redemption.

This is the paradox of the cross. The moment when God seemed most absent was actually the moment when God was most powerfully at work. The silence of heaven was not the silence of indifference but the silence of a love that was carrying the weight of the world's brokenness.

Through the suffering of Christ, God entered the darkest place of the human story and began the work of healing it from within.

Because Jesus entered that moment, the experience of abandonment no longer stands outside the reach of God's grace.

When believers cry out in confusion, they do not cry alone. The Son of God has already spoken those words, and the God who raised Jesus from the dead is still at work in the world even when His presence feels hidden.

There will still be moments when life does not make sense. There will still be times when prayers seem unanswered and faith feels fragile. But the cross assures us of something we might otherwise doubt.

God has not abandoned the world.

God has entered the world's deepest suffering.

The cry of Jesus reminds us that the darkest place in the human story has already been touched by the presence of God. And because of that, even the most painful questions can become part of our prayer.

"My God, my God, why have you forsaken me?"

Those words are not the end of faith.

They are the place where faith continues speaking to God in the darkness, trusting that the One who hears will one day bring resurrection out of the cross.

Chapter 9

Where Was God?

Text: Mark 15

OPENING PASTORAL SCENARIO: THE QUESTION PEOPLE WHISPER

Some questions are rarely asked in church, but they are asked everywhere else. Pastors hear them in hospital rooms, in quiet conversations after funerals, and in the moments when someone finally gathers the courage to speak honestly about suffering. The question usually comes slowly, often after a long pause.

"Where was God?"

People ask it after tragedy. They ask it after injustice. They ask it when suffering seems senseless and overwhelming. Sometimes the question comes through tears, sometimes with anger, and sometimes in a voice so quiet it almost feels dangerous to say it out loud.

But the question is real.

Where was God?

Many believers assume that faith requires avoiding that question. They worry that asking it might sound like doubt or accusation. They imagine that faithful people should respond to suffering with calm confidence, quickly affirming that God is present and in control.

Yet the Bible does not avoid this question. Scripture leads us directly to a moment when the question becomes unavoidable, and that moment appears in the story of the crucifixion.

Mark 15 describes the execution of Jesus. The scene unfolds slowly and painfully. Jesus is mocked by soldiers, ridiculed by religious leaders, and misunderstood by the crowds. Even the disciples who once followed Him closely have disappeared. The one who healed the sick, welcomed the outcast, and proclaimed the kingdom of God now hangs on a cross while the world watches.

From a human perspective, the scene feels deeply wrong.

The righteous one is condemned.
The innocent one suffers.
The one who embodied compassion and justice is treated as a criminal.

For anyone who believes that God governs the world with justice, the crucifixion raises an unavoidable question: Where was God?

The Gospels do not soften the disturbing nature of this moment. They describe it with remarkable honesty. The story does not appear neat or triumphant; it looks like the collapse of hope.

The disciples believed Jesus was the one who would restore Israel. They had seen miracles and heard Him speak about the coming kingdom of God. They had watched crowds gather around Him in amazement. Now the man they believed to be the Messiah is dying on a Roman cross.

The kingdom they expected does not appear.
The justice they hoped for does not arrive.
The promises they thought were unfolding now seem shattered.

From every human perspective, the crucifixion looks like defeat. Inside that moment the question grows louder.

Where was God?

This question represents another turning point in the biblical story we have been tracing throughout this book. Again and again Scripture confronts moments when the moral structure of the world appears to break. Abraham faced a command that seemed to contradict God's promise. Job struggled to understand why the righteous suffer. The psalmists cried out when God seemed silent. The writers of Lamentations tried to comprehend the destruction of Jerusalem.

Each of those moments revealed a fracture in the moral expectations of faith.

But the cross represents something even more profound. Here the one who perfectly embodied the character of God suffers the fate of the guilty. The teacher who spoke of mercy and justice is condemned by both religious and political authorities.

If there were ever a moment when the moral order of the world appeared broken, this is it.

This is why the cross stands at the center of the Christian story. It is not merely an example of suffering; it is the moment when the deepest questions about justice, faith, and the character of God converge.

When pastors approach Mark 15, they often emphasize the theological meaning of the cross. They speak about atonement, forgiveness, and redemption. These themes are essential to Christian faith. But before we move to those explanations, we must first recognize the raw experience described in the text itself.

The crucifixion looks like the triumph of injustice. The righteous one dies, the crowd mocks, the sky grows dark, and the Son of God breathes His last.

If we are honest, the question many people ask in moments of suffering echoes through this scene.

Where was God?

The answer to that question lies at the heart of the gospel, but it becomes visible only once we look closely at the rupture the cross represents.

THE PASSAGE AS WE USUALLY PREACH IT

When pastors preach the crucifixion, the focus often moves quickly toward its theological meaning. Sermons on Mark 15 usually emphasize what the cross accomplishes. The preacher explains that Jesus died for our sins, that His death brings forgiveness, and that through the cross God reconciles humanity to Himself.

These truths stand at the center of Christian faith. The New Testament repeatedly declares that the cross is the place where salvation is accomplished. Paul writes that Christ died for our sins according to the Scriptures, and Peter declares that Jesus bore our sins in His body on the tree. Because of this, sermons often move directly toward explanation and proclamation.

But in doing so, something important in the text itself can be overlooked.

Mark's Gospel does not begin with a theological explanation; it begins with a story. The evangelist carefully describes the events leading up to Jesus' death. The narrative unfolds step by step, revealing a scene that appears chaotic, unjust, and deeply troubling.

Jesus is arrested in the night and brought before religious authorities who search for accusations against Him. False witnesses testify, and the charges shift repeatedly. Eventually the leaders decide that Jesus must die. Yet they do not possess the authority to execute Him, so Jesus is brought before the Roman governor, Pontius Pilate.

Pilate questions Him while the crowd gathers and pressure builds. Although Pilate seems uncertain and appears to recognize something unusual about Jesus, he ultimately yields to the demands of the crowd and hands the innocent man over to be crucified.

From that moment the humiliation intensifies. Roman soldiers mock Jesus, dressing Him in a purple robe and placing a crown of thorns on His head. They kneel before Him in false reverence, shouting "Hail, king of the Jews!" before leading Him away to be executed (Mark 15:18).

The darkness of the narrative deepens as Jesus is taken to Golgotha. A cross is prepared, nails are driven into His hands and feet, and the execution takes place in public view. Above His head hangs a sign identifying the charge against Him: "The King of the Jews" (verse 26).

The irony is unmistakable. The one who proclaimed the kingdom of God now dies under a title meant to mock Him.

The mockery continues even as Jesus hangs on the cross. Passersby shake their heads and ridicule Him. Religious leaders join the taunting, challenging Him to save Himself if He truly possesses the power He claimed. Even the criminals crucified beside Him join the insults.

From every direction Jesus faces rejection and scorn.

When sermons move too quickly to theological explanation, the moral shock of this scene can be softened. But Mark's narrative invites the reader to feel the weight of what is happening.

The righteous one is condemned.
The innocent one suffers.
Those who should recognize the truth reject Him.
Those who should defend justice participate in injustice.

The entire scene feels disordered.

The crucifixion exposes the brokenness of the world in its rawest form. When we remain inside that moment, the deeper question of the passage becomes unavoidable.

Where was God?

THE MORAL INJURY QUESTION

At this point we ask the diagnostic question that guides this book:

Where does the moral world appear to break in this passage?

In Mark 15 the rupture is unmistakable. Everything about the scene feels inverted. The innocent is condemned, the righteous suffers, and those responsible for justice participate in injustice. Those who claim to speak for God reject the one who reveals God most clearly.

If there were ever a moment when the world stopped making moral sense, this is it.

Mark intentionally allows readers to feel that rupture. He does not rush past the injustice of the scene but carefully describes the layers of failure surrounding Jesus. Religious authority fails, political authority fails, and public opinion fails.

The systems that should uphold justice collapse.

From the perspective of moral expectation, the scene appears unbearable. If God is just, how can this happen? If God defends the righteous, why is the righteous one dying? If the kingdom of God has arrived in Jesus, why does the story end in execution?

These questions are not theoretical. They were already present in the minds of Jesus' followers. The disciples believed Jesus would restore Israel, yet the story now appears to end with Roman soldiers carrying out a public execution.

From every human perspective, the mission of Jesus seems to have failed.

This is what makes the crucifixion such a profound moment of moral rupture.

Earlier in Scripture we encountered moments when the moral order seemed strained. Job struggled to understand righteous suffering. The psalmists cried out when God seemed silent. The writers of Lamentations mourned the destruction of Jerusalem.

But the cross represents something deeper still.

Here the one who perfectly embodies the character of God suffers the fate of the guilty.

And the question echoes again:

Where was God?

WHAT THE MORAL INJURY LENS REVEALS

Once we recognize the rupture, the crucifixion begins to look different. Instead of moving quickly to explanation, we see the cross as the moment when the brokenness of the world is fully exposed.

The religious leaders fail.
Political authority fails.
The crowd fails.

Human systems collapse under the weight of fear, power, and self-interest. The innocent suffers, the guilty condemn, truth is ignored, and violence becomes normal.

The cross gathers the world's brokenness into a single moment.

Yet the cross also reveals something more profound. It reveals where God is when the moral world breaks.

God is not distant.

God is present.

The one suffering on the cross is the Son of God.

The answer to the question therefore becomes astonishing.

Where was God?

God was on the cross.

When the moral order collapses, God does not withdraw. God moves closer. Where injustice reigns, God is present. Where suffering overwhelms, God is present. Where the innocent suffer and the world seems broken beyond repair, God is present.

The cross becomes the place where the brokenness of the world and the love of God meet.

The world reveals its worst.

God reveals His heart.

HOW THE MORAL INJURY LENS CHANGES THE SERMON

Recognizing the rupture changes the way pastors preach this passage. Instead of beginning with explanation, the sermon begins with the question many people already carry.

Where was God?

This question is deeply pastoral. People in the congregation have asked it during grief, tragedy, injustice, and loss. When the preacher acknowledges that question honestly, the congregation recognizes that Scripture speaks to their experience.

The cross becomes more than doctrine.

It becomes the place where the deepest questions of the human heart are addressed.

The sermon allows the congregation to feel the rupture before offering an answer. Only then does the gospel reveal its response.

Where was God?

God was there.

God was not distant from suffering.

God was present in the suffering of Christ.

Because God entered the darkest place of human history, believers never face suffering alone. The cross reveals that when the moral world breaks, God does not retreat.

God steps into the rupture.

And from within that broken place, redemption begins.

SERMON - WHERE WAS GOD?

Text: Mark 15

Some questions are rarely spoken out loud in church, but they are asked everywhere else. They appear in hospital rooms where machines hum quietly beside a bed. They surface in long conversations after funerals, when the crowd has gone home and the silence finally settles in. They come late at night when a person sits alone, replaying the events that have shattered their world.

The question often arrives slowly. Sometimes it is whispered. Sometimes it comes through tears. Sometimes it comes with frustration or anger. But eventually the words form.

Where was God?

People ask that question when tragedy strikes without warning. They ask it when injustice seems to prevail. They ask it when suffering appears so senseless that no explanation seems large enough to hold it.

Where was God when the accident happened?
Where was God when the diagnosis came?
Where was God when violence shattered a community?
Where was God when everything fell apart?

Many believers feel uncomfortable asking that question. They assume that faith should prevent it. They imagine that faithful people should move quickly to confidence, quickly to reassurance, quickly to the declaration that everything will somehow work out.

But the Bible does not silence that question.

Instead, the Bible leads us directly to a moment where the question becomes unavoidable.

It leads us to the cross.

Mark 15 tells the story of Jesus' crucifixion with stark honesty. The narrative unfolds step by step, allowing us to see the scene as it happened. Jesus is arrested in the night, brought before religious leaders, and accused by witnesses whose testimonies do not agree. The charges shift until the leaders decide that Jesus must die.

But they cannot execute Him themselves. So Jesus is taken to the Roman governor, Pontius Pilate. Pilate questions Him and appears uncertain about what to do. Yet the pressure of the crowd grows stronger. The voices demanding execution become louder. Finally Pilate gives in.

The innocent man is handed over to be crucified.

From that moment the humiliation intensifies. Roman soldiers mock Jesus. They place a purple robe on His shoulders and twist together a crown of thorns, pressing it onto His head. They kneel before Him in mock reverence, shouting, "Hail, king of the Jews!" before leading Him away.

Jesus is taken to a place called Golgotha.

There the cross is prepared.

Nails are driven into His hands and feet.

The execution takes place in public view while people pass by and stare.

Above His head hangs a sign identifying the charge against Him: "The King of the Jews."

The sign is meant to mock Him, yet the reader knows something the crowd does not.

The title is true.

The one hanging on the cross really is the king.

But the mockery continues. Passersby shake their heads and insult Him. Religious leaders join the taunting. They challenge Him to save Himself if He truly possesses the power He claimed.

"He saved others," they say. "Let him save himself" (verse 31).

Even the criminals crucified beside Him heap insults upon Him.

From every direction Jesus faces rejection.

When we step back and look at this scene honestly, something about it feels deeply wrong.

The righteous one is condemned.
The innocent one suffers.
The one who embodied compassion and justice is treated like a criminal.

If God governs the world with justice, how can this happen?

And that question leads us back to the one many people ask in their own moments of suffering.

Where was God?

The crucifixion confronts us with the same tension that appears throughout Scripture. Again and again the Bible records moments when the moral order of the world seems to fracture. Abraham struggled to understand God's command concerning Isaac. Job could not reconcile his suffering with his righteousness. The psalmists cried out when God seemed silent. The writers of Lamentations mourned the destruction of Jerusalem.

Each of those moments raised questions about how the world works.

But the cross brings those questions to their most intense point.

Here the one who perfectly embodies the character of God suffers the fate of the guilty. The teacher who proclaimed mercy is condemned by religious authorities. The healer who brought restoration is executed by political power.

If there were ever a moment when the world stopped making moral sense, this is it.

And yet the Gospels do not attempt to soften the moment. They do not edit out the tension or hide the confusion. Instead, they tell the story exactly as it unfolded.

The righteous one dies.

The crowd mocks.

The sky grows dark.

And the Son of God breathes His last.

At this point the question becomes unavoidable.

Where was God?

Many people assume the answer must be that God was absent. When tragedy strikes, it can feel as though heaven has fallen silent. When injustice prevails, it can appear as though God has stepped away from the story.

But the cross reveals something very different.

God was not absent from this moment.

God was present in it.

The one hanging on the cross is the Son of God.

This means the answer to the question is both shocking and beautiful.

Where was God?

God was on the cross.

God was not watching from a distance.

God was entering the suffering of the world.

The cross reveals that God does not redeem the world from a safe distance. He does not observe human suffering as an outsider, offering sympathy from afar. Instead, God steps into the brokenness of the world personally.

The Son of God stands inside the darkest moment of human history.

He stands where injustice reigns.

He stands where violence triumphs.

He stands where the innocent suffer.

The cross reveals something astonishing about the character of God. When the moral structure of the world collapses, God does not withdraw.

God moves closer.

Where injustice appears, God is present.

Where suffering overwhelms, God is present.

Where the innocent suffer and the world seems broken beyond repair, God is present.

The cross becomes the place where the brokenness of the world and the love of God meet.

The world reveals its worst.

God reveals His heart.

This truth changes the way we think about suffering. Many people assume that if God were truly present, injustice would never succeed. They imagine that divine presence would prevent every tragedy and stop every act of cruelty.

But the cross shows that God's response to human suffering is not avoidance.

It is participation.

God enters the pain.

God bears the wound.

God stands inside the very place where human beings feel most abandoned.

The Son of God experiences rejection, humiliation, and agony. He stands beneath the weight of injustice. He absorbs the violence of the world rather than returning violence in response.

This means that when people ask, "Where was God when the world fell apart?" the answer of the gospel is not abstract.

God was there.

God was in Christ.

God was on the cross.

That does not remove the pain of suffering. It does not explain every tragedy or answer every mystery. But it reveals that the God Christians worship is not distant from human anguish.

He has entered it.

The God revealed in Jesus Christ is not untouched by grief or injustice. He knows them from the inside.

This is why the cross stands at the center of the Christian story. It reveals both the depth of the world's brokenness and the depth of God's love. The crucifixion shows how far human injustice can go, but it also shows how far God is willing to go to redeem the world.

God does not abandon the world when it becomes violent.

God does not retreat when the moral order collapses.

God enters the rupture.

He carries the weight of sin, injustice, cruelty, and suffering.

And through that act of self-giving love, something new begins.

The cross may look like defeat, but it is the beginning of redemption.

The darkness of Good Friday does not have the final word. The story will continue. Resurrection will follow. The one who appeared defeated will be revealed as victorious.

But before the victory becomes visible, the cross teaches us something essential about faith.

Faith does not ignore the brokenness of the world.

Faith looks directly at it.

Faith acknowledges the moments when life does not make sense. It recognizes the injustice, the grief, the confusion, and the unanswered questions.

And then faith discovers something remarkable.

God is present even there.

When believers ask the question that rises in moments of suffering—Where was God?—the cross gives an answer that is both sobering and hopeful.

God was not absent from the suffering.

God entered it.

God stood in the darkest place of the human story.

And because God entered that place, the brokenness of the world does not have the final word.

The God who was present on the cross is also the God who raises the dead.

The God who entered the rupture of the world is the God who heals it.

The God who stood with the suffering is the God who brings resurrection.

So when the question rises again—and it will rise again—the cross allows the church to answer with honesty and hope.

Where was God?

God was there.

God was in Christ.

God was on the cross.

And because He was there, even the darkest places of our world are not beyond the reach of redemption.

Chapter 10

The Morning the World Began Again

Text: John 20

OPENING PASTORAL SCENARIO: WHEN HOPE FEELS IMPOSSIBLE

There are moments when people stop expecting anything good to happen.

The loss has already occurred. The damage is done. The future that once seemed possible has vanished, and life becomes a slow process of learning how to live with disappointment. In those moments people no longer ask why something happened because they no longer believe the answer would change anything.

They simply assume that the story has ended.

Pastors encounter this quiet despair more often than many people realize. A widow sits in the pew where she once worshiped beside her husband and wonders what the coming years will look like. A family struggles to rebuild life after a devastating loss. A person who once prayed with confidence now approaches faith cautiously, unsure whether hope is safe anymore.

What makes these moments especially difficult is not only the pain itself.

It is the feeling that nothing new can happen.

People reach a point where they assume the future holds nothing more than survival. The world has already revealed what it is capable of taking away. The future feels smaller than the past. Life continues, but hope feels fragile.

This emotional landscape forms the background of John 20.

By the time we reach this chapter, the disciples of Jesus are living inside what appears to be the end of their story. The crucifixion has shattered everything they believed about the future. The one they trusted as the Messiah has died publicly and violently. The movement they thought would transform the world now seems finished.

The disciples are not expecting resurrection.

They are expecting to survive grief.

This detail matters because Christians often read the resurrection story too quickly. We know how the story ends, so it is easy to imagine that the disciples somehow anticipated what was coming. But the Gospel narratives make it clear that no one expected the resurrection.

The disciples were not waiting for Easter morning.

They were mourning.

The events of the previous days had created the deepest moral rupture imaginable. The one who embodied goodness had been condemned. The one who healed others had been executed. The one who spoke about the kingdom of God had died under the authority of Rome.

From every human perspective, the story had collapsed.

The moral expectations that shaped the disciples' understanding of the world had been shattered. If Jesus truly was the Messiah, how could He be executed like a criminal? If God was truly at work through Him, why had heaven remained silent?

The cross had not only taken Jesus' life.

It had taken the disciples' sense of meaning and direction.

This is the emotional world we enter when John tells the story of Easter morning.

Mary Magdalene arrives at the tomb while it is still dark. John emphasizes this detail deliberately. Darkness still surrounds the scene, reflecting the emotional state of those who loved Jesus. The grief of the crucifixion has not yet lifted.

Mary is not coming to celebrate a miracle.

She is coming to mourn.

Her expectation is painfully simple. Jesus is dead, and she wants to honor His body with the care that love offers even when hope has vanished. But when she arrives at the tomb, something unexpected has happened.

The stone has been rolled away.

Her immediate reaction is not hope but confusion. She assumes someone has moved the body. She runs to tell Peter and the other disciple, trying to make sense of what she has seen.

In that moment Mary's response reflects a deeply human instinct. When the world has already broken once, people do not immediately expect restoration. They search for explanations that match the brokenness they have already experienced.

Perhaps someone took the body.

Perhaps the authorities moved it.

Perhaps something else has happened.

But resurrection is the last possibility anyone considers.

This is one of the reasons the resurrection story carries such power. It does not begin with confident faith. It begins with confusion, grief, and uncertainty. The disciples are not celebrating victory. They are struggling to understand what the future holds after their world has collapsed.

The moral injury lens helps us recognize the significance of this moment.

Throughout this book we have traced the pattern of moral rupture in Scripture. Again and again the biblical story confronts moments when the moral order of the world appears to break. Abraham faced the unthinkable command to sacrifice Isaac. Job suffered without explanation. The psalmists cried out in lament. The prophets mourned the destruction of Jerusalem.

At the cross the rupture reached its deepest point.

The Son of God died while heaven appeared silent.

If the story ended there, the cross would represent the final collapse of hope.

But John 20 tells us the story does not end there.

The resurrection introduces something entirely new into the human story. It reveals that the moment that looked like ultimate defeat was not the end of God's work after all.

Yet the beauty of this chapter lies in the way the resurrection unfolds gradually.

It begins quietly.

A stone moved.

A tomb empty.

A woman weeping in a garden.

John invites us to enter the story slowly, allowing the shock of resurrection to emerge step by step. The first moments of Easter morning do not resemble the triumphant scenes we sometimes imagine. They unfold in the quiet confusion of grief that has not yet turned into joy.

Mary stands outside the tomb and weeps.

She still believes death has won.

In that moment she represents every human being who has experienced the collapse of hope. She stands in the place where grief feels final and the future feels uncertain.

And then something happens that changes everything.

Before we follow the story further, however, we must pause and consider how this passage is usually preached.

THE PASSAGE AS WE USUALLY PREACH IT

When pastors preach the resurrection, the tone is usually one of celebration and victory. Easter Sunday is the most joyful day in the Christian calendar. Churches fill with music, flowers, and hopeful expectation. The message of the sermon often centers on the triumph of life over death and the victory of Christ over sin and the grave.

And rightly so.

The resurrection stands at the center of Christian faith. The apostle Paul writes that if Christ has not been raised, our faith is futile. Everything Christians believe about salvation, forgiveness, and eternal life rests on the reality that Jesus rose from the dead.

Because the resurrection carries such importance, sermons about Easter often focus on proclaiming that victory clearly and confidently. The preacher announces that death has been defeated. The grave could not hold Christ. The power of God has broken through the darkness of Good Friday.

The message is bold and triumphant.

Christ is risen.

Yet when we focus exclusively on the victory of the resurrection, we sometimes move too quickly past something important in the way the story actually unfolds.

John 20 does not begin with celebration.

It begins with grief.

Mary Magdalene arrives at the tomb not anticipating resurrection but mourning a loss she believes is permanent. When she sees the stone rolled away, she does not interpret the moment as hope. She assumes someone has taken the body.

Peter and the other disciple run to the tomb. They see the burial cloths lying there, but even this does not immediately produce clarity. John tells us they still did not understand that Jesus must rise from the dead.

Eventually they return home.

Mary remains behind.

She stands outside the tomb and weeps.

Before the risen Christ appears, John allows us to sit inside this moment of grief. Mary bends down to look into the tomb and sees two angels sitting where Jesus' body had been. They ask her a simple question.

"Woman, why are you weeping?" (John 20:13).

Her answer reveals the depth of her sorrow.

"They have taken away my Lord, and I do not know where they have laid him" (verse 13).

Mary's world still looks exactly like the world of Good Friday. The loss feels final. The confusion remains unresolved.

Hope has not yet returned.

Only after this moment does the resurrection begin to reveal itself.

THE MORAL INJURY QUESTION

At this point we ask the diagnostic question that guides this book.

Where does the moral world appear to break in this passage?

In earlier chapters the rupture occurred in the event itself. Abraham faced an impossible command. Job suffered unjustly. The cross shattered the moral logic of the world.

But in John 20 the rupture has already happened.

The disciples are living in the aftermath.

The cross has destroyed the expectations that once shaped their faith. Everything they believed about Jesus and the future now feels uncertain. The one they trusted is dead.

The kingdom they expected has not arrived.

The story they believed God was writing now appears finished.

Mary approaches the tomb from within that moral collapse. Her grief is not only emotional but theological. If Jesus truly was the Messiah, how could this happen?

If God was truly present in His ministry, why did God allow this?

These are the kinds of questions people ask whenever the moral order of the world collapses.

When tragedy strikes unexpectedly, people feel disoriented. The assumptions that once guided life suddenly feel unreliable.

Mary stands in that place.

She believes the story has ended.

And it is precisely there that the resurrection begins.

WHAT THE MORAL INJURY LENS REVEALS

When we read John 20 through the lens of moral injury, something remarkable appears.

The resurrection is not merely a miracle that reverses death.

It is God's answer to the deepest rupture in the moral structure of the world.

The cross looked like the final collapse of hope. The righteous one died while injustice appeared to triumph.

But the resurrection reveals that the story was not finished.

The first person to encounter the risen Christ is Mary Magdalene, standing alone in a garden, weeping beside an empty tomb. She does not recognize Him at first. She assumes He is the gardener.

Then Jesus speaks a single word.

"Mary."

In that moment everything changes.

Recognition dawns. The one she believed dead now stands alive before her.

This moment reveals something profound about the character of resurrection.

God answers moral rupture not with explanation but with presence.

Jesus does not begin with a lecture about the meaning of His resurrection. Instead, He restores relationship. The one who mourned now hears her name spoken in love.

The resurrection therefore reveals the beginning of new creation.

The setting of the story reinforces this truth.

The resurrection occurs in a garden.

The biblical story began in a garden where humanity lived in communion with God. After the fall that harmony was broken. Now, in another garden, something new begins.

The resurrection marks the start of a new creation.

The world that seemed broken beyond repair has begun again.

Mary arrived believing the story had ended.

She leaves as the first witness that the story has begun again.

HOW THIS CHANGES THE SERMON

When pastors preach the resurrection, the instinct is often to begin with celebration.

But John 20 begins with grief.

The moral injury lens reminds us that many people sitting in church live in a world that still feels like Good Friday. They carry losses that have reshaped their understanding of the future.

If the sermon begins only with triumph, those listeners may struggle to connect with the message.

But when the sermon begins with Mary weeping outside the tomb, something changes.

People recognize themselves in the story.

The resurrection does not ignore the collapse of hope.

It begins inside it.

Mary stands in the place where she believes the story has ended.

Then Jesus calls her name.

This moment reveals the heart of Easter.

The risen Christ meets people where they mourn.

He speaks into the places where hope has died.

And from that place, the story begins again.

SERMON - THE MORNING THE WORLD BEGAN AGAIN

Text: John 20

There are moments in life when people stop expecting anything good to happen. The loss has already occurred, the damage is done, and the future that once seemed full of possibility has disappeared. Life continues, but it feels smaller than it once did. Hope becomes something fragile, something approached cautiously rather than embraced with confidence.

Many people learn to live this way after suffering. A family that has endured devastating loss begins to structure life around what is missing. A person who once prayed with certainty begins to pray more carefully, uncertain whether hope is safe anymore. Someone who once believed the future would unfold in meaningful ways now focuses mostly on getting through the next day.

In those moments people do not always ask why something happened. They simply assume that the story has ended.

That is the emotional world we encounter at the beginning of John 20.

When the Gospel tells us that Mary Magdalene came to the tomb early in the morning while it was still dark, the detail is more than a description of time. It reflects the spiritual atmosphere surrounding the disciples after the crucifixion. Darkness still defines the story. The grief of Good Friday has not lifted. The future that once seemed full of promise has collapsed.

Mary does not come to the tomb expecting a miracle. She comes because love requires one final act of care. The one she followed and trusted has died, and the only thing left to do is honor His body.

This is important because we sometimes imagine that the first Easter morning began with believers waiting expectantly for resurrection. But the Gospels make it clear that no one anticipated what God was about to do. The disciples were not preparing to celebrate victory. They were learning how to live with grief.

The crucifixion had shattered everything they believed about the future. Jesus had spoken about the kingdom of God, about restoration and redemption, about the transformation of the world. The disciples had seen miracles, heard His teaching, and watched people respond with amazement.

But now He was dead.

The one who healed others had not been rescued from suffering Himself. The one who spoke about the power of God had died under the authority of Rome. The one who seemed to embody the hope of Israel had been executed as a criminal.

From every human perspective, the story had ended.

This is why Mary's reaction when she reaches the tomb is so revealing. When she sees that the stone has been rolled away, she does not assume resurrection. She assumes that someone has taken the body.

Her mind searches for an explanation that fits the broken world she has just experienced. Death has already claimed its victory, so the empty tomb must mean something else.

She runs to Peter and the other disciple and tells them what she believes has happened. They rush to the tomb and see the linen cloths lying there, but even this does not immediately produce understanding. John tells us that they did not yet understand that Jesus must rise from the dead.

Eventually the disciples return home.

Mary remains behind.

She stands outside the tomb and weeps.

This moment matters because it reveals something about the way hope often returns after suffering. When the moral world collapses, people do not immediately regain their confidence in the future. Even when something new begins to happen, grief can make it difficult to recognize.

Mary's tears represent the experience of countless people who feel as though the best chapters of their story are already finished. She believes that the most she can do now is mourn what has been lost.

Then something extraordinary happens.

Mary looks into the tomb and sees two angels sitting where Jesus' body had been. They ask her a simple question: "Woman, why are you weeping?"

Her answer shows how deeply grief has shaped her understanding of reality.

"They have taken away my Lord, and I do not know where they have laid him."

In that moment the story still looks exactly like Good Friday.

Mary turns and sees someone standing nearby. John tells us that it is Jesus, but she does not recognize Him. She assumes He is the gardener and asks if He has moved the body somewhere else.

Then Jesus speaks a single word.

"Mary."

That word changes everything.

The voice she knows so well breaks through her grief, and suddenly the truth becomes visible. The one she believed dead now stands before her alive.

"Rabboni," she cries.

Teacher.

This moment is one of the most beautiful scenes in all of Scripture. The resurrection is not first announced to a crowd of powerful leaders or proclaimed before the religious authorities who condemned Jesus. It is revealed to a grieving woman standing alone in a garden.

The turning point of the human story begins with a name spoken in love.

When Jesus says "Mary," the relationship that seemed destroyed on Good Friday is restored. Death has not ended the story. The injustice of the cross has not silenced the work of God. The silence of the tomb has been broken.

This is the moment when the world begins again.

To understand the significance of this moment, we must remember the moral rupture that preceded it. Throughout Scripture we have seen moments when the moral order of the world appeared to break. The righteous suffered. Injustice triumphed. Heaven seemed silent.

At the cross that rupture reached its deepest point. The Son of God died while the world mocked and the sky grew dark.

If the story ended there, the cross would represent the final collapse of hope.

But the resurrection reveals something that no one expected.

God was still working.

The moment that looked like ultimate defeat was actually the doorway through which God was bringing life into the world in a new way.

The resurrection is not merely a miracle that reverses death. It is the declaration that the moral collapse of Good Friday does not define the future of creation.

The power of death is real, but it is not final.

The injustice of the world is real, but it is not ultimate.

The grief that Mary carried to the tomb is real, but it is not permanent.

In the garden on Easter morning, God begins the work of new creation.

This is why the setting of the resurrection matters so much. John tells us that the encounter between Mary and Jesus takes place in a garden. That detail echoes the very beginning of the biblical story.

In Genesis, humanity's story begins in a garden where life flourishes in communion with God. When sin enters the world, that harmony is broken. Humanity is driven out of the garden, and the world becomes a place marked by suffering, death, and moral confusion.

Now, in another garden, something new begins.

The resurrection is the beginning of a new creation.

The world that seemed permanently damaged by sin and injustice is being restored. The story that appeared to end in death begins again with life.

But notice how gently this new creation begins.

There are no crowds yet.

There are no trumpets.

There is only a grieving woman and the voice of the risen Christ speaking her name.

This reveals something important about how God works in the world. The transformation of creation does not begin with overwhelming displays of power. It begins with restoration of relationship.

Jesus calls Mary by name.

That detail speaks deeply into the experience of people who live with moral injury. When the moral order of the world collapses, people often feel forgotten. They wonder whether their suffering places them outside the reach of God's attention.

The resurrection answers that fear.

The risen Christ knows our names.

He meets people in the places where they believe the story has ended. Mary expected only grief, but she encountered the living Christ who had already begun a new chapter.

The same truth remains central to the Christian message today.

There are moments when individuals and communities feel as though their world has collapsed. Loss, injustice, violence, and grief can create the impression that hope has disappeared from the future.

But the resurrection declares that the story of the world is not finished.

The God who raised Jesus from the dead continues to work in the places where hope seems impossible.

This does not mean that suffering is erased. Even after the resurrection, the wounds of the cross remain visible on Jesus' body. Redemption does not erase the past.

It transforms it.

The risen Christ carries the marks of crucifixion, showing that the brokenness of the world has been taken into the life of God Himself.

This is why Easter does not ignore Good Friday.

It redeems it.

The suffering that appeared meaningless becomes the place where God reveals the depth of divine love. The injustice that seemed final becomes the doorway through which resurrection enters the world.

Mary arrived at the tomb believing the story had ended.

She left as the first witness that the story had begun again.

And that is the message the resurrection continues to proclaim.

The morning that began in darkness became the morning when the world itself began again.

Where grief had defined the future, hope appeared.

Where death seemed final, life emerged.

Where the story looked finished, God began writing a new chapter.

The resurrection declares that the deepest rupture in the moral fabric of the world has not defeated the purposes of God.

Instead, God has begun the work of making all things new.

And that work began in a garden, with a name spoken in love, on the morning when the world began again.

PART IV

LIVING IN A WOUNDED WORLD

Chapter 11

Blessed Are Those Who Mourn

Text: Matthew 5:1–12

OPENING PASTORAL SCENARIO: WHEN GRIEF CHANGES THE WAY WE SEE THE WORLD

There are moments in life when grief quietly reshapes the way people see everything.

The loss may come suddenly, or it may unfold slowly over time. A loved one dies. A relationship breaks apart. A tragedy occurs that no one could have predicted. In the days and weeks that follow, the world begins to look different.

Things that once felt certain now feel fragile.

People who have experienced deep grief often describe a strange sensation: life continues around them, but they feel as though they are living in a different world. Conversations move on to ordinary topics while their own hearts remain fixed on the loss that has changed everything.

The laughter of others can feel distant. Simple routines take more effort than they once did. Even faith can feel different. The prayers that once came easily now feel heavier—sometimes quieter, sometimes filled with questions that were never asked before.

Pastors encounter this reality frequently.

Someone sits in the church office after a funeral and says something that reveals how deeply their world has shifted.

"I don't see things the same way anymore."

They do not mean that they have lost faith. In fact, many grieving people cling to faith more deeply than ever. But grief has opened their eyes to the brokenness of the world in a way they had not fully seen before.

They notice suffering more quickly.

They feel the pain of others more deeply.

They realize how fragile life can be.

And sometimes they quietly wonder whether their sorrow places them outside the happiness they once associated with faith.

When people read the words of Jesus in the Beatitudes, that question can feel especially sharp.

"Blessed are the poor in spirit."
"Blessed are those who mourn."
"Blessed are the meek" (Matt 5:3–5).

At first glance those words sound strange.

Blessed are those who mourn?

Most people associate blessing with joy, prosperity, or success. When we imagine a blessed life, we picture happiness, stability, and good fortune.

Mourning does not seem to belong in that picture.

Grief feels like the opposite of blessing.

Yet Jesus begins His most famous sermon with precisely this declaration. Standing before a crowd gathered on a hillside, He describes the people whom God calls blessed.

And surprisingly, many of them are people who are hurting.

The poor in spirit.

Those who mourn.

Those who hunger and thirst for righteousness.

Those who are persecuted.

Jesus' description of blessing does not match the expectations most people carry about what a good life looks like. Instead, His words turn those expectations upside down.

Why would Jesus call mourners blessed?

To understand that question, we need to remember the world in which Jesus spoke these words.

The people gathered to hear Him were not living comfortable lives. Many of them lived under the heavy weight of Roman rule. Political power rested in the hands of an empire that had little concern for their welfare. Economic hardship was common. Illness and poverty touched many families.

In addition to these struggles, many faithful Jews carried a deep sense of disappointment about the state of their world. The promises of God's kingdom had not yet been fulfilled in the way they expected. Injustice still existed. Oppression still shaped daily life.

Many longed for a world that looked more like the one God had promised.

In other words, the audience listening to Jesus knew something about mourning.

Some mourned personal losses. Others mourned the brokenness of their nation. Still others mourned the injustice they saw around them and wondered when God would finally set things right.

Into that world Jesus speaks a surprising declaration.

"Blessed are those who mourn, for they shall be comforted" (verse 4).

Those words carry enormous weight when we consider them carefully. Jesus is not dismissing grief. He is not pretending that sorrow is pleasant or desirable. Mourning remains painful.

But Jesus insists that those who mourn are not outside the reach of God's blessing.

They are closer to it than they realize.

This insight becomes especially meaningful when we view the Beatitudes through the lens of moral injury.

Throughout this book we have explored moments when the moral order of the world appears to break. Abraham faced the unthinkable command to sacrifice Isaac. Job struggled to understand why the righteous suffer. The psalmists cried out when God seemed silent.

Again and again the Bible confronts the experience of people whose expectations about justice and goodness have been shattered.

Mourning often grows out of those moments.

When people experience moral rupture, they grieve. They grieve the loss of what should have been. They grieve the suffering they see in the world. They grieve the gap between the goodness they believe God intends and the brokenness they experience every day.

Jesus does not condemn that grief.

He calls those people blessed.

The Beatitudes reveal something profound about the heart of God. God's blessing does not belong only to those who appear successful or happy. It belongs especially to those who recognize that the world is not yet what it should be.

Those who mourn see the brokenness of the world clearly.

And because they see it clearly, they are open to the comfort that only God can bring.

This perspective transforms the way we understand both grief and blessing. Mourning is not evidence that faith has failed. It is often the sign that faith is taking the brokenness of the world seriously.

Those who mourn are people whose hearts are awake to the suffering around them.

And Jesus says that such people are not forgotten.

They are blessed.

In the next section we will explore how this passage is usually preached and why the moral injury lens allows us to see a deeper meaning in Jesus' words about mourning and comfort.

THE PASSAGE AS WE USUALLY PREACH IT

When pastors preach the Beatitudes, the emphasis often falls on the beauty of Jesus' vision for life in God's kingdom. These opening words of the Sermon on the Mount are among the most familiar teachings in the New Testament, and they carry a tone many people find deeply comforting.

Jesus describes the people who are blessed by God.

The poor in spirit.

Those who mourn.

The meek.

Those who hunger and thirst for righteousness.

The merciful.

The pure in heart.

The peacemakers.

In many sermons, the Beatitudes are presented as a description of the character God desires in His people. The message often focuses on the virtues Jesus highlights—humility, mercy, purity, and the pursuit of peace. The preacher encourages the congregation to cultivate these qualities as evidence of belonging to God's kingdom.

This approach captures an important dimension of the text.

The Beatitudes do describe the character of those who follow Christ. They present a picture of a life shaped by humility, compassion, and trust in God rather than by pride or self-sufficiency. In this sense, the Beatitudes function as an introduction to the ethical teaching that follows throughout the Sermon on the Mount.

But when we read the Beatitudes only as a list of virtues to pursue, something subtle happens.

We begin to hear Jesus' words primarily as instructions.

The people He calls blessed begin to sound like people who have already achieved these qualities. The poor in spirit are humble believers. The merciful are those who actively show compassion. The peacemakers are those who work to bring reconciliation.

The Beatitudes become a description of the kind of life we should strive to live.

While there is truth in that interpretation, it can obscure the emotional and social context in which Jesus first spoke these words.

Consider the second Beatitude in particular:

"Blessed are those who mourn, for they shall be comforted."

In many sermons, this verse is interpreted primarily as sorrow over personal sin. Yet when we step back and consider the wider context of Jesus' ministry, mourning likely carries a broader meaning.

Jesus is speaking to a crowd familiar with suffering.

Many live in poverty. Some have experienced illness or loss. Others carry the weight of political oppression. Many also mourn the condition of their nation and long for God's promised restoration.

Their mourning is not only personal.

It is moral and communal.

They grieve the brokenness of the world.

When we recognize this dimension of mourning, the Beatitudes begin to sound less like spiritual advice and more like a proclamation of hope for people living in a wounded world.

Jesus does not dismiss their grief.

He declares that those who mourn are blessed.

THE MORAL INJURY QUESTION

At this point we ask the diagnostic question that has guided our reading throughout the book:

Where does the moral world appear to break in this passage?

The answer emerges in the presence of mourning itself.

People mourn because something that should have been whole has been broken. Something that should have been right has gone wrong.

When a loved one dies, we mourn because death does not feel natural to the human heart. When injustice harms the innocent, we mourn because we believe the world should be governed by justice and compassion.

Mourning reveals the gap between the world as it is and the world as it should be.

That gap lies at the center of moral injury.

Moral injury occurs when a person's deepest expectations about goodness, justice, or faithfulness collide with experiences that violate those expectations. Something happens that should not happen. A promise fails. Innocent people suffer.

The moral structure of reality appears to crack.

The Beatitudes speak directly into that experience.

Jesus recognizes that many people live with this tension between God's promises and the world's brokenness.

And He declares that those who mourn are blessed.

WHAT THE MORAL INJURY LENS REVEALS

When we read the Beatitudes through the lens of moral injury, the passage begins to look different.

The Beatitudes are not merely a list of virtues.

They are a description of people whose hearts have been awakened by the brokenness of the world.

Those who mourn are people who see the fracture clearly.

They recognize that the present world is not yet what God intends it to be. Their grief reflects a longing for the restoration that God has promised.

This mourning therefore reveals moral awareness.

People mourn because they still believe goodness matters.

They mourn because they refuse to accept injustice as normal.

They mourn because they believe God intends something better for the world.

Jesus looks at those mourners and calls them blessed.

Their grief does not separate them from God's blessing.

It prepares them to receive it.

HOW THE MORAL INJURY LENS CHANGES THE SERMON

When pastors see the Beatitudes through this lens, the tone of preaching changes.

The passage is no longer simply a call to develop certain virtues. It becomes a word of hope spoken directly into the wounds people carry.

Instead of beginning with moral instruction, the sermon begins by acknowledging the reality of grief. It recognizes the sorrow present in the congregation and reminds listeners that mourning is not foreign to the life of faith.

Scripture itself gives voice to lament.

The psalmists cry out in grief.

The prophets mourn injustice.

Even Jesus weeps.

When the sermon acknowledges this reality, mourners discover that their grief has not placed them outside the story of God's people.

They are standing exactly where many faithful people in Scripture have stood before them.

From that place the promise of Jesus becomes visible.

"Blessed are those who mourn, for they shall be comforted."

The sermon does not rush past grief.

It allows the congregation to remain inside the tension long enough to hear the promise clearly.

God has not forgotten those who mourn.

Their grief will not be the final word.

The comfort Jesus promises points toward the restoration God intends for the world.

Those who mourn now are people who long for that restoration.

And Jesus declares that they are blessed.

The sermon that follows explores how this promise of comfort speaks to those who live with grief today and how the Beatitudes reveal the surprising way God meets people in the midst of a broken world.

SERMON - BLESSED ARE THOSE WHO MOURN

Text: Matthew 5:1–12

There are moments in life when grief quietly changes the way people see the world. Something happens that cannot be undone, and from that moment forward life feels different. A loved one dies. A relationship ends. A tragedy unfolds that no one could have predicted. In the days that follow, the world begins to look unfamiliar.

People often describe this experience in very similar ways. They say that life continues around them as if nothing has changed, but they feel as though they are living in a different world. Conversations move on to ordinary topics while their own hearts remain fixed on the loss that has altered everything.

Things that once felt certain now feel fragile. Plans that once seemed obvious now feel uncertain. Even faith can feel different. Prayers may still be spoken, but they carry a different weight. Sometimes they are quieter, sometimes more honest, sometimes filled with questions that were never asked before.

Pastors encounter this reality frequently. Someone sits across the desk in a church office after a funeral or after a painful experience and says something that reveals how deeply their world has shifted.

"I don't see things the same way anymore."

Often they worry that something has gone wrong in their faith. They wonder whether grief has somehow placed them outside the experience of blessing that they once associated with following God. When life hurts deeply, it can be difficult to reconcile that pain with the promises of faith.

That tension makes the words of Jesus in the Beatitudes sound almost surprising.

"Blessed are the poor in spirit, for theirs is the kingdom of heaven.
Blessed are those who mourn, for they shall be comforted."

Blessed are those who mourn.

At first hearing, those words feel strange. Most people associate blessing with happiness, prosperity, or success. When we imagine a blessed life, we picture stability, joy, and good fortune. Mourning does not seem to belong in that picture.

Grief feels like the opposite of blessing.

Yet Jesus begins His most famous sermon with precisely this declaration. Standing before a crowd gathered on a hillside, He describes the people whom God calls blessed. And surprisingly, many of them are people who are hurting.

The poor in spirit.

Those who mourn.

Those who hunger and thirst for righteousness.

Those who are persecuted.

Jesus' description of blessing does not match the expectations most people carry about what a good life should look like. Instead, His words turn those expectations upside down.

To understand why Jesus calls mourners blessed, we need to think about the people who were standing before Him that day.

The crowd gathered on the hillside did not consist of comfortable people living easy lives. Many of them were poor. Many carried the burdens of illness or economic hardship. All of them lived under the rule of the Roman Empire, a political system that offered little concern for their welfare.

Beyond these personal struggles, many faithful Jews also carried a deep sense of disappointment about the condition of their world. They believed that God had promised to restore Israel and establish His kingdom in righteousness. Yet their present reality seemed far from that promise.

Injustice persisted. Oppression continued. The world did not yet look the way they believed God intended it to be.

Many of them mourned.

Some mourned personal losses. Others mourned the brokenness of their nation. Still others mourned the injustice they saw around them and wondered when God would finally set things right.

Into that world Jesus speaks these astonishing words.

"Blessed are those who mourn, for they shall be comforted."

Jesus does not dismiss their grief. He does not tell them that mourning is unnecessary or that faithful people should simply feel happier. Instead, He acknowledges their sorrow and then makes a remarkable declaration.

Those who mourn are blessed.

To understand this, we need to recognize something about the nature of mourning itself. People mourn because they believe something precious has been lost. They mourn because something that should have been whole has been broken.

When someone we love dies, we mourn because we know that human life is meant for more than death. When injustice harms the innocent, we mourn because we believe the world should be governed by justice and compassion. When violence or cruelty damages lives, we mourn because we instinctively know that human beings were not created to live this way.

Mourning reveals the gap between the world as it is and the world as it should be.

The Bible consistently affirms that this longing for goodness reflects something true about the nature of creation. Human beings were created in the image of God, and that means we carry within us a deep awareness that goodness matters.

We know that justice should prevail.

We know that love should endure.

We know that suffering should not have the final word.

When those expectations collide with a broken world, people grieve.

Throughout Scripture we see faithful people wrestling with this tension. Abraham struggled to understand the command to sacrifice Isaac. Job cried out in confusion when suffering entered his life. The psalmists lamented when God seemed silent.

Their mourning did not represent a failure of faith.

It represented faith taking the brokenness of the world seriously.

This is the context in which Jesus calls mourners blessed.

Those who mourn are people whose hearts remain awake to the pain of the world. They have not become numb to suffering. They have not convinced themselves that injustice is normal. They have not stopped longing for the goodness they believe God intends.

Their grief reveals that they still believe the world should be different.

In that sense, mourning can be a deeply spiritual response to moral rupture. When people encounter suffering that should not exist, their grief expresses a refusal to accept that brokenness as the final reality of the world.

Jesus sees those mourners standing before Him and declares that they are blessed.

Not because sorrow itself is pleasant, but because their grief places them within the reach of God's promise.

"Blessed are those who mourn, for they shall be comforted."

The promise of comfort is crucial here. Jesus does not say that mourners will remain trapped in sorrow forever. He points toward a future moment when God's comfort will answer the grief they carry.

That promise runs throughout the biblical story. The prophets spoke about a day when God would wipe away tears and restore justice to the earth. They described a future when brokenness would be healed and the suffering of the present age would give way to the restoration of creation.

Jesus' words in the Beatitudes echo that promise.

Those who mourn now are people who long for that future.

They hunger for righteousness. They desire a world where goodness prevails and injustice is healed. Their grief is not the absence of faith but the expression of hope that refuses to accept the brokenness of the world as final.

In this way, mourning and hope become deeply connected.

Those who mourn are people who believe that the world should be better than it is. They believe that God's goodness remains real even when the present moment feels dark. Their grief reflects a longing for the day when God's kingdom will fully arrive.

The life of Jesus Himself reveals how deeply God shares that longing.

Jesus does not remain distant from the suffering of humanity. The Gospels tell us that He wept at the tomb of Lazarus. He grieved over the city of Jerusalem. He carried the sorrow of a wounded world in His own heart.

Ultimately, that grief led Him to the cross.

There, the brokenness of the world reached its most painful expression. The innocent Son of God suffered injustice while heaven seemed silent. The moral rupture of the world appeared complete.

Yet the story did not end there.

The resurrection revealed that the suffering of the cross was not the final chapter. God was already at work bringing life out of the deepest darkness.

That same hope lies behind the promise Jesus speaks in the Beatitudes.

Those who mourn shall be comforted.

The comfort Jesus promises is not shallow reassurance. It is the restoration of the world that God has always intended. It is the healing of the wounds that mourning exposes. It is the moment when justice and mercy meet and the brokenness of creation is finally made whole.

For people who live with grief today, this promise carries profound meaning.

Many believers quietly wonder whether their sorrow places them outside the experience of blessing. They assume that faithful people should always appear joyful or confident. When their hearts feel heavy, they worry that something must be wrong with their faith.

But Jesus' words challenge that assumption.

Those who mourn are not excluded from blessing.

They are included in it.

Their grief reveals that they still believe goodness matters. Their sorrow reveals that they still long for the world God intends to create. Their mourning is a sign that their hearts remain aligned with the hope of God's kingdom.

Jesus looks at those mourners and calls them blessed.

Not because the world is already healed, but because God's promise of comfort is already on its way.

The kingdom of heaven belongs to those who recognize that the world is not yet what it should be.

The blessing of God rests upon those whose hearts remain open to the brokenness around them.

And one day, the comfort Jesus promised will arrive.

On that day the mourning of the present age will give way to the restoration of creation. Tears will be wiped away. Justice will prevail. The broken things of the world will be made whole again.

Until that day, the words of Jesus remain a source of profound comfort for those who grieve.

Blessed are those who mourn.

For they shall be comforted.

Chapter 12

Hope in a Groaning World

Text: Romans 8

OPENING PASTORAL SCENARIO: WHEN THE WORLD FEELS HEAVIER THAN IT SHOULD

There are seasons in life when the weight of the world feels unusually heavy.

The news carries stories of violence, war, and injustice. Communities face tragedies that leave families grieving and searching for answers. Personal struggles—illness, loss, financial uncertainty, fractured relationships—add to the quiet burdens people already carry.

In those moments the world can begin to feel different.

People still go to work, attend church, and move through the routines of daily life, but beneath the surface there is a growing awareness that something about the world is not the way it should be.

A parent watches a child suffer from an illness that medicine cannot fully heal. A family stands beside a hospital bed wondering how long their loved one has left. A community mourns the loss of lives taken far too soon.

These experiences create a strange mixture of emotions.

Grief and hope exist side by side.

Faith remains present, but it often feels more fragile than before.

People continue to believe that God is good, yet the world around them sometimes makes that goodness difficult to understand.

Pastors encounter this tension regularly.

After a funeral someone quietly asks, "Why does life have to be this way?"

Another person confesses that they believe in God but struggle to understand why suffering seems so common.

Others express the feeling in simpler terms.

"The world feels broken."

These words reflect a deep moral awareness.

Human beings instinctively recognize that suffering, injustice, and death do not belong to the world as it should be. Something in the human heart resists the idea that the present condition of creation represents its final form.

We know that life was meant for more.

This awareness appears throughout Scripture.

The writers of the Bible repeatedly confront the tension between the goodness of God and the brokenness of the world. The psalmists cry out when injustice seems to prevail. The prophets mourn the suffering of their people. Even Jesus Himself weeps at the tomb of Lazarus.

The apostle Paul addresses this tension directly in one of the most remarkable passages in the New Testament.

Romans 8 describes the condition of creation using a powerful image.

The world, Paul says, is groaning.

Creation itself longs for restoration. Humanity groans under the weight of suffering. Even believers groan as they wait for the redemption God has promised.

Yet within that groaning Paul speaks of hope.

Understanding this tension between groaning and hope is essential for preaching in a wounded world.

THE PASSAGE AS WE USUALLY PREACH IT

Romans 8 is one of the most beloved chapters in the New Testament. Pastors often turn to it when preaching about assurance, the work of the Spirit, or the promise that nothing can separate believers from the love of God.

The chapter begins with a declaration that has brought comfort to countless Christians:

"There is therefore now no condemnation for those who are in Christ Jesus."

From there Paul unfolds a sweeping vision of life in the Spirit. He speaks about freedom from the power of sin, the adoption of believers as children of God, and the assurance that God is at work in all things for the good of those who love Him.

The chapter culminates in one of the most triumphant passages in Scripture.

Nothing in all creation, Paul declares, will be able to separate us from the love of God in Christ Jesus our Lord.

When sermons focus on these themes, Romans 8 becomes a proclamation of confidence and assurance. The preacher emphasizes the victory believers possess through Christ and the security of God's love.

These truths stand at the heart of the Christian message.

Yet when we move too quickly to the triumphant conclusion of the chapter, we sometimes overlook the section that stands in the middle of Paul's argument.

Before Paul speaks about unshakable confidence, he speaks about groaning.

Creation groans.

Believers groan.

The Spirit Himself intercedes with groanings too deep for words.

This language reveals something important about Paul's understanding of the Christian life.

Faith does not remove the experience of suffering.

Believers still live within a world that feels unfinished.

The redemption Christ has accomplished has already begun, but the final restoration of creation has not yet arrived.

Romans 8 therefore describes life in the tension between promise and fulfillment.

It is the tension between the world as it is and the world as God intends it to be.

THE MORAL INJURY QUESTION

At this point we ask the question that has guided our reading throughout this book:

Where does the moral world appear to break in this passage?

In Romans 8 the rupture appears in the condition of creation itself.

Paul writes that creation has been subjected to frustration. The natural world no longer functions in the harmony that God originally intended. Suffering, decay, and death have entered the fabric of life.

Creation groans.

Human beings groan as well.

We experience the pain of illness, loss, injustice, and death. Even believers who possess the firstfruits of the Spirit feel the weight of this brokenness.

Paul does not deny this reality.

He names it.

The groaning of creation reveals that the present condition of the world is not the way it was meant to be.

Something has gone wrong.

This recognition aligns closely with what we have described throughout this book as moral rupture. Human beings sense that the world is out of joint. The suffering we encounter feels incompatible with the goodness we believe God intends.

Romans 8 acknowledges this tension openly.

Paul does not pretend that believers live in a world where everything already makes sense.

Instead, he describes a creation that longs for redemption.

WHAT THE MORAL INJURY LENS REVEALS

When we read Romans 8 through the lens of moral injury, the chapter begins to reveal a profound theological insight.

The groaning of creation is not a sign that faith has failed.

It is evidence that the world is unfinished.

Paul describes believers as people who possess the "firstfruits of the Spirit" (Rom 8:23). In agricultural language, the firstfruits represent the earliest portion of a harvest that promises more to come.

The Spirit's presence within believers therefore represents the beginning of a restoration that has not yet been completed.

Christ's resurrection has already begun the renewal of creation.

But the world still waits for its full redemption.

This is why groaning and hope exist side by side.

Creation groans because it longs for the freedom that will come when God restores all things. Believers groan because they recognize that the present world does not yet reflect the fullness of God's promise.

Yet this groaning is not despair.

It is longing.

Paul compares the groaning of creation to the pains of childbirth. This metaphor is important. The pain of childbirth does not signal the end of life but the arrival of new life.

The suffering of the present age therefore points toward a future restoration.

The moral injury lens helps us see that Romans 8 does not deny the brokenness of the world.

Instead, it places that brokenness within a larger story.

The groaning of creation is the sound of a world waiting to be made new.

HOW THE MORAL INJURY LENS CHANGES THE SERMON

When pastors preach Romans 8 with this perspective in mind, the tone of the sermon often changes.

Instead of rushing directly to the triumphant conclusion of the chapter, the preacher acknowledges the reality of the groaning that Paul describes.

The sermon recognizes the suffering present in the congregation.

People sitting in the pews know what it means to groan.

They groan when illness touches their families.

They groan when injustice harms the vulnerable.

They groan when grief leaves an empty place in their lives.

When the sermon names this experience honestly, listeners recognize that Scripture understands the world they inhabit.

Romans 8 does not ask believers to pretend that suffering is insignificant.

It acknowledges the weight of living in a world that is still waiting for redemption.

Yet the passage also proclaims hope.

The groaning of creation does not mean that God has abandoned the world.

It means that the story is still unfolding.

The Spirit intercedes for believers.

Christ intercedes for the saints.

And the God who began the work of redemption will bring it to completion.

Preaching shaped by this vision offers something deeply needed in a wounded world.

It tells the truth about suffering without surrendering hope.

The sermon that follows explores this tension between groaning and hope more fully.

SERMON - HOPE IN THE GROANING WORLD

Text: Romans 8

There are moments in life when the weight of the world feels heavier than it should. Something happens that exposes the fragility of life, and suddenly the world does not look quite the same. A diagnosis arrives that no one expected. A phone call in the middle of the night brings news that changes everything. A tragedy appears on the evening news and reminds us that suffering is never far away.

In those moments people often find themselves thinking the same quiet thought. Something about the world feels wrong. The way things are does not seem to match the way things should be.

Human beings have an instinctive awareness that life was meant for more than this. We know that suffering does not belong. We know that injustice is not the way the world was intended to function. We know that death interrupts something sacred about the gift of life.

When those realities confront us, the world can begin to feel like a place that is out of joint. People still go to work. Children still play in the yard. Life continues in familiar ways. Yet beneath the surface there is a growing awareness that something deep within creation is unsettled.

The apostle Paul gives language to that experience in one of the most remarkable passages in the New Testament. In Romans chapter eight, Paul describes the condition of the world with a single powerful image.

Creation, he says, is groaning.

The image is striking because it is so honest. Paul does not describe the world as peaceful or harmonious. He does not pretend that suffering is rare or insignificant. Instead, he speaks of creation itself as though it were a living thing crying out under the weight of something it was never meant to bear.

The world groans.

Human beings groan.

Even believers who know the presence of the Spirit within their lives feel the ache of that groaning.

Paul writes that the whole creation has been groaning together as in the pains of childbirth until now. The language suggests something deep and universal. The suffering we experience is not isolated or random. It belongs to a world that is still waiting for something.

Creation itself is waiting for redemption.

This is one of the most important truths Scripture teaches about the world we inhabit. The present condition of creation is not the final form of God's work. The world as we experience it now is not the world as God ultimately intends it to be.

Something has gone wrong.

The Bible tells us that the creation was subjected to frustration. The harmony that once defined the world has been disrupted. Decay has entered the fabric of life. Death interrupts the story of every human being.

The world groans because it is wounded.

We see that groaning in many places. We see it when illness touches someone we love. We see it when injustice harms the vulnerable. We see it when violence destroys lives that should have been allowed to flourish.

We see it when grief sits quietly beside us and reminds us that someone we loved is no longer here.

These experiences are not simply unfortunate accidents within an otherwise perfect system. They are signs that the world itself is longing for something that has not yet arrived.

The apostle Paul understands this longing.

He says that creation waits with eager expectation for the revealing of the children of God. In other words, the world itself anticipates the day when God will restore what has been broken.

This idea can be difficult for modern readers to grasp because we often think of salvation only in personal terms. We think about forgiveness, about heaven, about our relationship with God. All of these things are important, but Paul reminds us that God's plan of redemption is far larger than the salvation of individual souls.

God intends to restore the entire creation.

The world that now groans under the weight of suffering will one day experience freedom. The decay that shapes our present reality will not last forever. The brokenness that causes grief and confusion will not define the future.

Creation itself waits for the day when God completes the work of renewal.

Yet Paul does not say that believers stand outside this groaning world. He does not suggest that faith lifts us above the experience of suffering. Instead, he tells us that we groan as well.

Even those who possess the firstfruits of the Spirit, Paul says, groan inwardly as we wait for adoption as sons and daughters, the redemption of our bodies.

This means that the Christian life is lived in the tension between promise and fulfillment.

Something extraordinary has already happened. Through the death and resurrection of Jesus Christ, God has begun the renewal of creation. The resurrection is the first sign that death will not have the final word.

Yet the completion of that renewal has not yet arrived.

We live in the middle of the story.

We live in the time between the resurrection and the final restoration of the world. The power of God's redemption is already at work, but the fullness of that redemption is still ahead.

This is why groaning and hope exist together in the Christian life.

We groan because we recognize that the world is not yet what it should be. We see suffering that should not exist. We encounter loss that feels unbearable. We experience injustice that cries out for correction.

At the same time, we hope because we know that the story is not finished.

Paul describes hope in a way that challenges many of our assumptions. He writes that hope that is seen is not hope at all. If we can already see the fulfillment of a promise, then hope is no longer necessary.

Hope exists precisely because the fulfillment has not yet arrived.

Christian hope is therefore not the denial of suffering. It is not a refusal to acknowledge the pain of living in a broken world. Instead, hope is the conviction that suffering does not have the final word.

Hope believes that God is still at work even when the present moment feels uncertain.

Paul goes even further and tells us that the Spirit of God enters the experience of our groaning. When we do not know how to pray, when words fail to capture the depth of what we feel, the Spirit intercedes for us with groanings too deep for words.

This is one of the most tender images in all of Scripture.

It reminds us that God does not stand at a distance from our suffering. The Spirit enters the silence of our confusion and carries our prayers before the throne of God.

There are moments in life when prayer feels easy. Words come naturally, and faith feels steady. But there are also moments when prayer feels almost impossible.

Grief can make language feel inadequate. Loss can leave us staring at the ceiling in the middle of the night, unsure of what to say to God. In those moments the promise of Romans eight becomes especially precious.

Even when we cannot find the words, the Spirit prays for us.

God understands the groaning of the human heart.

This truth reminds us that our suffering does not place us outside the reach of God's presence. The groaning we experience is not evidence that God has abandoned us. It is part of living in a world that is still waiting for redemption.

Paul concludes this section of Romans eight with a promise that has carried believers through centuries of hardship.

We know, he writes, that in all things God works for the good of those who love him, who have been called according to his purpose.

This verse is often misunderstood. It does not mean that every event in life is good. Scripture never suggests that suffering itself is good. Illness, injustice, and death remain enemies of the life God intended for creation.

What Paul means is something deeper.

God is able to work within every circumstance of life to bring about His redemptive purposes.

Even the moments that seem most broken are not outside the reach of God's power.

The clearest example of this truth is the cross.

If there were ever a moment when the world appeared to collapse morally, it was the crucifixion of Jesus. The one who embodied goodness and truth was condemned and executed by the powers of the world.

From every human perspective, the cross looked like defeat.

Yet the resurrection revealed that God had been at work even in that moment. The place where hope seemed to die became the place where new creation began.

The same God who brought resurrection out of the ruins of Good Friday continues to work in the world today.

This does not mean that suffering disappears from our lives. It means that suffering cannot separate us from the love of God.

That truth becomes the triumphant conclusion of Romans eight.

Paul asks a series of questions that echo across the centuries. If God is for us, who can be against us? Who shall separate us from the love of Christ?

Shall trouble or hardship or persecution or famine or nakedness or danger or sword?

Paul answers his own questions with breathtaking confidence.

No, in all these things we are more than conquerors through him who loved us.

The confidence Paul expresses here is not based on the belief that life will always be easy. His own life proves the opposite. Paul endured imprisonment, persecution, and hardship.

Yet he remained convinced that none of these experiences could sever the bond between believers and the love of God.

Neither death nor life, neither angels nor rulers, neither things present nor things to come, nor powers, nor height nor depth, nor anything else in all creation will be able to separate us from the love of God in Christ Jesus our Lord.

This promise speaks directly into the groaning of the world.

The suffering we experience does not have the authority to rewrite the story God is telling. The brokenness of the present age does not cancel the hope of redemption.

Creation may groan.

Human hearts may groan.

But the love of God remains stronger than every force that threatens to overwhelm us.

This means that the groaning of the present world is not the final sound of the story.

The final sound will be the joy of a creation restored.

One day the work God began through the resurrection of Jesus will reach its completion. The decay that touches every corner of the world will be replaced by life. The injustice that wounds communities will give way to righteousness.

The grief that fills our hearts will be replaced by joy.

Until that day arrives, we continue to live in the tension between groaning and hope.

We groan because we recognize the brokenness of the world.

We hope because we know the story is not finished.

And the God who began the work of redemption will one day bring it to completion.

That is the hope we carry into a groaning world.

And it is the hope that sustains the people of God.

Conclusion

The God Who Hears the Cry

Throughout this book we have walked through some of the most difficult passages in Scripture. We began in Deuteronomy 30, where the world appears morally ordered and coherent. Covenant faithfulness leads to blessing, and disobedience leads to judgment. It is the world as people hope it will be—a world where justice makes sense and righteousness matters.

But very quickly the biblical story complicates that expectation.

In Genesis 22, Abraham faces the unthinkable command to sacrifice the son through whom God's promise was supposed to come. In that moment the moral structure of Abraham's world collapses. The God who promised life now seems to demand death.

In Job, the collapse becomes even more explicit. A righteous man suffers devastating loss while his friends struggle to defend a system of easy explanations. Job's protest reveals that faith sometimes survives not by understanding everything but by refusing to let go of God even when the world stops making sense.

The Psalms deepen this honesty. In Psalm 13, the psalmist cries out, "How long, O Lord?" The prayer gives voice to the frustration of waiting for God in a world where injustice and suffering seem to linger. In Psalm 22, the language becomes even more stark: "My God, my God, why have you forsaken me?"

These words are not whispered quietly on the margins of Scripture.

They are preserved at the center of Israel's prayer life.

Then we moved into the catastrophe of Lamentations, where the destruction of Jerusalem forces an entire community to confront the collapse of the world they believed God had promised them. Yet even there, in the middle of grief, the writer declares:

"The steadfast love of the Lord never ceases;
his mercies never come to an end" (Lam 3:22).

Hope appears not outside the ruins but within them.

The story reaches its most dramatic point at the cross.

When Jesus cries out the words of Psalm 22—"My God, my God, why have you forsaken me?"—He enters fully into the experience of moral rupture that has echoed throughout Scripture. The Son of God stands within the deepest place of human confusion and suffering.

At that moment the moral tension of the entire biblical story converges.

If the righteous sufferer of Job raised questions about divine justice, the crucifixion intensifies those questions beyond anything previously imagined. The one Christians proclaim as the Messiah dies under the power of imperial violence.

From a purely human perspective, the cross appears to confirm the collapse of moral order.

Yet the resurrection reveals something astonishing.

God has not abandoned the world.

Instead, God has entered the brokenness of the world in order to redeem it.

When we arrive at John 20, the resurrection does not erase the wounds of the crucifixion. Jesus still bears the marks of suffering in His hands and side. But those wounds have been transformed. They are no longer signs of defeat; they are signs that death itself has been overcome.

The resurrection does not deny the reality of moral rupture.

It announces that rupture will not have the final word.

That truth carries enormous significance for the church today.

Many people who enter a sanctuary on Sunday morning are quietly wrestling with experiences that have disrupted their understanding of the world. They have seen suffering that appears unjust. They have endured losses that seem impossible to explain. They have encountered moments when faith felt fragile.

Often these experiences remain unspoken.

People may assume that their questions are inappropriate in a setting where faith is expected to appear confident and steady. They may wonder whether their confusion places them outside the life of faith.

But the biblical story tells a different story.

From Abraham to Job, from the psalmists to the prophets, from the disciples to the apostle Paul, Scripture repeatedly shows us people who encountered God precisely in moments when the moral order of their world seemed to collapse.

The Bible does not hide those moments.

It gives them language.

This insight lies at the heart of the moral injury lens we have explored throughout this book.

Moral injury occurs when a person's deeply held understanding of how the world should work is violated. It is not simply the experience of suffering;

it is the experience of disorientation that follows when suffering appears to contradict our moral expectations.

Many people carry this kind of wound.

They may not use the term moral injury, but they know what it feels like to face events that challenge their sense of justice, goodness, and meaning.

When pastors preach Scripture with this reality in mind, something important begins to happen.

Congregations discover that the Bible speaks directly to the world they inhabit.

The psalms of lament become more than ancient poetry. They become prayers that give voice to emotions many people have struggled to express. The story of Job becomes more than a theological puzzle; it becomes a companion for those wrestling with undeserved suffering. The cross becomes more than a doctrinal statement about atonement; it becomes the place where God enters the deepest wounds of human experience.

Preaching shaped by this lens does not eliminate the tension of life.

Instead, it allows Scripture to address that tension honestly.

Such preaching names the rupture people see in the world while also proclaiming the hope revealed in Christ. It acknowledges that faith sometimes includes confusion, grief, and protest, but it also announces that these experiences do not lie outside the reach of God's redemption.

In fact, they are often the very places where redemption becomes visible.

This perspective also reshapes the vocation of the preacher.

Pastors are not merely communicators of theological information. They are witnesses to the ways God meets people in the midst of a wounded world. The pulpit becomes a place where Scripture interprets the fractures of human experience and reveals the presence of Christ within them.

When congregations hear sermons that speak honestly about suffering while still proclaiming the hope of the gospel, they often discover a deeper connection between faith and life.

The church becomes a place where people can bring their questions without fear. It becomes a community where lament is not silenced but welcomed, and where hope grows not from denial but from the promise of God's faithfulness.

Ultimately the message of Scripture is not that the world always makes sense.

The message is that God remains faithful even when the world does not.

The biblical story moves from creation to covenant, from lament to exile, from cross to resurrection, and finally toward the promise of a renewed creation where justice and peace will be fully restored.

That final vision appears in the closing pages of the Bible.

The book of Revelation describes a future in which God dwells with humanity and wipes away every tear. Death, mourning, crying, and pain are no more, because the old order of things has passed away.

The promise of that future does not erase the wounds of the present.

But it assures us that those wounds are not the end of the story.

The God who met Abraham on the mountain, who listened to Job's protest, who heard the psalmists' cries, who walked with the disciples on the road to Emmaus, and who raised Jesus from the dead is the same God who continues to meet His people today.

He meets them in hospital rooms and quiet living rooms.
He meets them in moments of prayer and in seasons of doubt.
He meets them in churches where pastors faithfully proclaim the gospel.

And He meets them even in the ruins of a world that sometimes feels broken beyond repair.

This is the hope that Christian preaching ultimately announces.

Not that life will always make sense.

But that the God revealed in Jesus Christ walks with us when it does not.

And because He walks with us, the story of the world is still moving toward redemption.

Even now.

Acknowledgments

Every book has a story behind it, and this one is no different. Although a single name appears on the cover, the ideas, encouragement, and conversations that shaped these pages came from many people whose influence deserves recognition.

First, I give thanks to God, whose patience with His people is far greater than our understanding of Him. The Scriptures explored in this book are filled with voices that cry out in confusion, protest, and hope. Writing these chapters reminded me again and again that the Bible does not hide the wounds of the world. Instead, it reveals the God who meets us within them. For that truth, and for the grace that continues to sustain the church through every generation, I am deeply grateful.

I am also thankful for the congregations I have had the privilege of serving. Pastoral ministry has a way of bringing a preacher face to face with the realities that theology books sometimes discuss only in theory. People carry burdens into church every week—grief, disappointment, unanswered questions, and quiet fears about the future. Many of the insights explored in this book emerged not in academic settings but in conversations with individuals seeking to understand how faith survives when life becomes difficult. Their courage in sharing their stories helped shape the pastoral heart behind these pages.

My gratitude also extends to fellow pastors and ministry colleagues who continue to wrestle faithfully with the challenge of preaching the gospel in a complicated world. Preachers know that every sermon stands at the intersection of Scripture and human experience. The conversations we have had—about difficult passages, about suffering in our communities, about the challenge of proclaiming hope without ignoring reality—have deeply influenced the ideas explored in this book.

I am grateful as well for the many biblical scholars, theologians, and writers whose work has shaped my understanding of Scripture. Though this book is written primarily for pastors rather than academic specialists, it stands on the shoulders of generations of careful scholarship. Their efforts to illuminate the biblical text have helped make it possible for pastors to proclaim the Scriptures with clarity and confidence.

Special thanks are also due to friends and family who have encouraged this project from its earliest stages. Writing a book requires time, patience, and the willingness to return again and again to ideas that are still taking shape. Their support made it possible to continue the work when the process felt slow or uncertain.

Finally, I want to acknowledge the countless people—both within and beyond the church—who are searching for hope in a world that sometimes feels deeply broken. Many carry questions about suffering, injustice, and loss that cannot be answered with simple explanations. This book is written with them in mind.

My prayer is that pastors who read these pages will find encouragement to preach the Scriptures with honesty and courage, and that congregations who hear those sermons will discover again that the God revealed in Jesus Christ is not distant from the wounds of the world.

He meets us in the midst of them.

About the Author

Rev. G. C. Smith, PhD, is a pastor, clinical pastoral counselor, and writer whose work focuses on the intersection of biblical interpretation, trauma, grief, and pastoral ministry. His calling has centered on helping the church speak faithfully to people whose lives have been shaped by suffering, loss, and experiences that challenge their understanding of the world.

Rev. Smith holds a PhD in Clinical Pastoral Counseling, with a specialty in trauma and grief. His academic work and clinical training have focused on the ways deep moral and emotional wounds shape human experience and spiritual life. Through this work he has explored how the concept of moral injury—often discussed in trauma studies—can illuminate many of the most difficult passages in Scripture.

Alongside his academic training, Rev. Smith has served in pastoral ministry, preaching and walking with individuals and families through seasons of loss, crisis, and spiritual questioning. Those pastoral experiences convinced him that many people enter church carrying wounds that traditional sermons do not always address directly. Questions about injustice, suffering, betrayal, and grief often remain unspoken, leaving many believers unsure how faith speaks to the most difficult moments of life.

His work seeks to help pastors and congregations rediscover the Bible's remarkable honesty about these realities. Throughout Scripture, figures such as Abraham, Job, the psalmists, the prophets, and the disciples themselves encounter moments when the moral structure of the world appears to collapse. Rather than avoiding these tensions, the biblical narrative gives them voice through lament, protest, and prayer.

Drawing on both biblical theology and pastoral counseling, Rev. Smith developed what he describes as a moral injury hermeneutic—a way of reading Scripture that highlights how the Bible addresses moments when deeply held moral expectations are violated. This approach reveals how the biblical story repeatedly moves from moral rupture toward divine presence and ultimately toward redemption.

In *Preaching Scripture When the Moral World Collapses*, Rev. Smith brings together his experience in pastoral ministry and trauma-informed counseling to offer a practical resource for preachers. The book demonstrates how reading Scripture through the lens of moral injury can deepen interpretation, enrich preaching, and help congregations encounter the gospel in the midst of life's most difficult experiences.

Rev. Smith remains committed to the life of the church, the faithful proclamation of Scripture, and the pastoral calling to bring hope to a world that is often wounded yet never beyond the reach of God's redeeming grace.

www.ingramcontent.com/pod-product-compliance
Lightning Source LLC
LaVergne TN
LVHW020536100826
845148LV00010B/1479

* 9 7 9 8 3 8 5 2 8 2 5 7 9 *